Just Think

Performance Task - Grade 6

for the Primary Exit Profile (PEP)® Examination

STRATEGIC AND EXTENDED THINKING

Christine Fearon Levene

LMH PUBLISHING LIMITED

© 2020, LMH Publishing Limited
First Edition
10 9 8 7 6 5 4 3 2 1

All rights reserved. No part of this book may be reproduced, stored in a retrieval system, or transmitted, in any form or by any means, electronic, mechanical, photocopying, recording, or otherwise, without the expressed written permission of the publisher or author.

The publishers have made every effort to trace the copyright holders, but if they have inadvertently overlooked any, they will be pleased to make the necessary arrangements at the first opportunity.

These materials may contain links for third party websites. We have no control over, and are not responsible for the contents of such third party websites. Please use care when accessing them.

If you have bought this book without a cover, you should be aware that it is "stolen" property. The publisher(s)/author(s) have not received any payment for the "stripped" book, if it is printed without their authorization.

All LMH titles, imprints and distributed lines are available at special quantity discounts for bulk purchases for sales promotion, premiums, fund-raising, educational or institutional use.

Written and Compiled: Mrs. Christine Fearon Levene
Edited by: Dr. A. Mandara
Cover design, book design and formatting: Roshane Mullings

Published by: LMH Publishing Limited
Suite 10-11
Sagicor Industrial Park
7 Norman Road
Kingston C.S.O., Jamaica
Tel.: 876-938-0005; Fax: 876-759-8752
Email: lmhbookpublishing@cwjamaica.com
Website: www.lmhpublishing.com

ISBN: 978-976-8245-80-9

NATIONAL LIBRARY OF JAMAICA CATALOGUING-IN-PUBLICATION DATA

Names: Levene, Christine Fearon, author
Title: Just think : performance task – Grade 6 for the Primary
    Exit Profile (PEP) Examination / Christine Fearon Levene.
Description: Kingston : LMH Publishers, 2020. | Audience : Grade
    6 | Ages 11-12.
Identifiers: ISBN 9789768245809 (pbk).
Subjects: LCSH: English language – Examinations, questions, etc.
    | Mathematics – Examinations, questions, etc. | Curriculum-
    based assessment. | Critical thinking – Ability testing.
Classification: DDC 372.6 -- dc23.

Preface

Just Think Performance Task is a workbook designed to meet the needs of Grade 6 students who will sit Mathematics and Language Arts performance tasks, one of the three components of the PEP examination.

The performance task is an activity or assessment that asks students to solve a problem by demonstrating their knowledge, understanding and proficiency. It is curriculum based and assesses students' grasp of concepts, principles and procedures coming from the content of language arts and mathematics.

In language arts, students' ability to gather information from multiple sources will be assessed. Students will be assessed in reading, writing and research from the following areas of the curriculum: Grammar and Convention, Comprehension, Vocabulary, Research/Study Skills and Extended Writing (narrative, expository, persuasive and descriptive compositions). The extended writing may also include preparing a report about a study, or writing a letter to an editor to or about a previous publication or about a product.

In mathematics, students will be assessed at higher order levels which require strategic and extended thinking. The use of analytical and problem solving skills along with evaluation are vital to effectively complete these tasks. This begs for the application of different strands of mathematics in real world scenarios.

This book provides age-appropriate practice on topical issues. It engages students in the development of written communication and critical thinking skills. The book seeks to develop and enhance the communication skills and creativity for the 21st century learner. Some items provide the opportunity for students to think creatively as they seek to persuade a specific audience using support which enhances their research skills. Other tasks encourage them to take multiple approaches to solving a problem.

There are 30 tasks (15 mathematics and 15 language arts) each with four to six items as suggested by the Ministry of Education. There is a variety of items aimed at improving students' confidence in this component of the examination.

Educators, we trust that you will use this book as a platform to further develop students' written communication skills along with their ability to apply content learnt to real life situations by providing them with similar activities.

Parents/Guardians, use this book as a guide to the pathway to help students realize the importance or relevance of the school curriculum to real life. Create your own items and have candid discussions about how and what they are doing in school is used in practical ways.

Students, you may be worried about the exam but there is no need for that. There is good news! The necessary **skills can be developed with practice**. The purpose of this book is to improve your critical thinking and communication skills while developing a passion for such items. Enjoy!

Contents

Section 1 - Mathematics

Task One	1
Task Two	5
Task Three	7
Task Four	11
Task Five	13
Task Six	16
Task Seven	18
Task Eight	21
Task Nine	25
Task Ten	27
Task Eleven	31
Task Twelve	33
Task Thirteen	36
Task Fourteen	39
Task Fifteen	42

Section 2 - Language Arts

Skills	45
Context Clues	47
Task One	51
Task Two	58
Task Three	64
Task Four	69
Task Five	73
Task Six	78
Task Seven	82
Task Eight	90
Task Nine	96
Task Ten	103
Task Eleven	109
Task Twelve	115
Task Thirteen	120
Task Fourteen	128
Task Fifteen	135
Rubric for Extended Writing Tasks: Narratives	141
Rubric for Persuasive Writing	144
Rubric for Expository Writing	147

Section 1 - Mathematics

Task One

Your class and your teacher are going on a trip. There are three possible choices: **Kool Runnings Water Park**, **Simon Bolivar Museum**, and **Hope Zoo**. Your teacher asked students to write down their first choice. In this task, you will determine where the class should go on the field trip based on the survey results and the cost per student. This is a picture of your school and the three different locations.

TASK ONE

After a discussion, the students agreed to allow everyone to vote for the place he/she prefers to visit. They would all attend the trip even if it is not their preference.

The class voted on which place to visit. This table shows the results.

STUDENT	CHOICE	STUDENT	CHOICE
Dante	Waterpark	Patrick	Waterpark
Kristen	Waterpark	Simone	Waterpark
Julia	Waterpark	Keano	Waterpark
Sean	Zoo	Ramani	Waterpark
Krista	Waterpark	Tavina	Waterpark
Kemar	Museum	Deanna	Waterpark
Shauna Kay	Waterpark	Jada	Waterpark
Jayden	Waterpark	Arianne	Museum
Dora	Museum	Aria	Waterpark
Oliver	Museum	Alex	Waterpark
Jevon	Waterpark	Roy	Museum
Gabrielle	Waterpark	Andy	Waterpark
Cameron	Museum	Naheem	Zoo
David	Zoo	Paris	Waterpark
Christian	Zoo	Jaheim	Waterpark

Here is some additional information.

- The class teacher and her assistant do not pay an entrance fee to any of the destinations as two adults are allowed free entry if there are 24 or more students. Teachers will not contribute to the bus fare.
- There are 30 students in the class.
- Only 1 bus is needed.
- The bus charge is for the entire bus load of students (not for each passenger).
- Each student will pay the same amount.
- The driver charges $600 for each kilometre to destinations in Kingston and St. Andrew. For other parishes there is a flat charge of $54000.

Destination	Parish	Distance from school	Entry fee per person
Kool Runnings Water Park	Hanover	108 km	$1500
Simon Bolivar	Kingston	20 km	$300
Hope Zoo	St. Andrew	30 km	$200

TASK ONE

Activity 1

Based only on the class votes, where will the class go on the trip? Explain the reason for your selection.

_____
_____
_____
_____
_____
_____
_____
_____

Activity 2

How much will <u>each</u> student pay to go on each trip? Show your work, or explain how you found your answer.

Kool Runnings Adventure Park	Simon Bolivar Museum	Hope Zoo
$	$	$

TASK ONE

Activity 3

David thinks that it will cost less to go to the zoo because the entrance fee is only $200 per person. Explain why you agree or disagree with David's thinking.

_____
_____
_____
_____
_____
_____
_____
_____
_____
_____

Activity 4

Write a short note to your teacher stating where you think the class should go on its field trip, based on how you would evaluate all the different factors, including student votes, costs, distance, and what you think would be fun.

_____
_____
_____
_____
_____
_____
_____
_____
_____
_____

Task Two

Mr. Woodstock has a plot of land **36** metres long and **16** metres wide. He uses the land for mixed farming – rearing animals and growing crops.

1. What length of wire does Mr. Woodstock need to fence his land?

   _____
   _____
   _____
   _____

2. How much surface does the plot of land cover?

   _____
   _____
   _____
   _____

3. If 1 m^2 of matted grass is sold for $38, how much money would Mr. Woodstock need to cover his land space?

   _____
   _____
   _____
   _____
   _____

TASK TWO

4. Mr. Woodstock uses half of his land for rearing animals, one-quarter for vegetables and the remaining portion as an orchard. Using the scale 1cm = 4m, prepare a floor drawing of the plot of land and how it is used. **Ensure that all measurements are accurate. Label each section as is given in the information. Colour each section in a different colour and create a key.**

Key:

Task Three

Areas: Measurement and Statistics

Below is a plan of Mr. Hamilton's Farm. The shaded area shows how he uses the land. One side of each small square represents 1 metre.

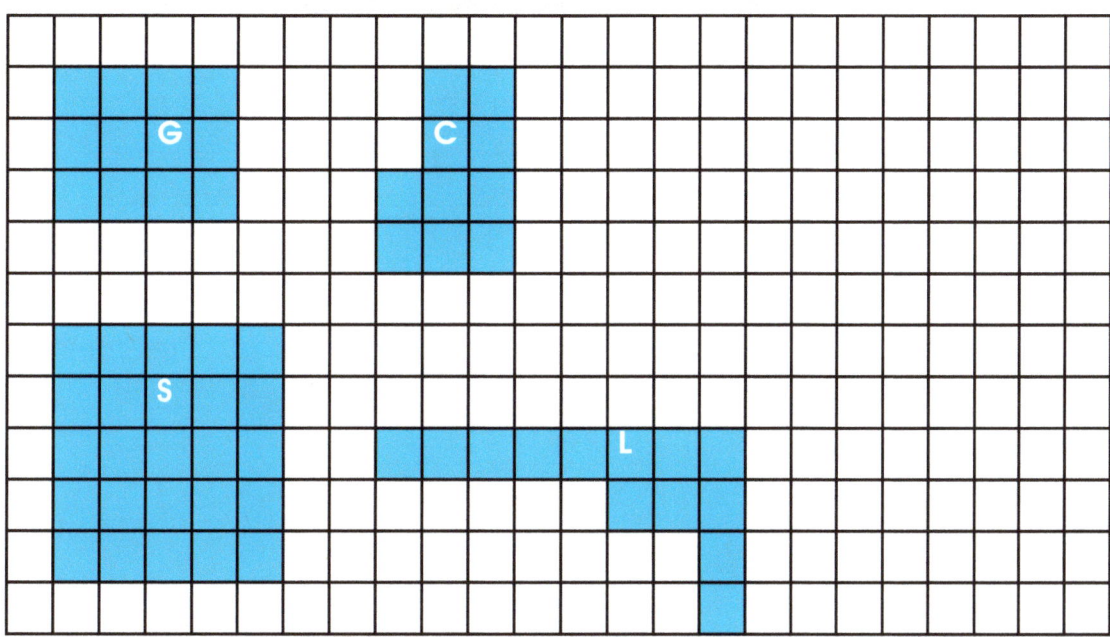

G – animal grazing   **C** – cucumber
L – lettuce   **S** – sweet potato

1. What is the area of the section designated for planting sweet potatoes?

_____
_____
_____
_____
_____
_____

TASK THREE

2. What is the perimeter of **C**?

   _____
   _____
   _____
   _____

3. If another rectangle identical to figure **G** was placed immediately to its right without gaps or overlaps, what would be the perimeter of the new figure?

   _____
   _____
   _____
   _____

4. Mr. Hamilton decides to fence the section assigned to animal grazing.
   a) What would he calculate to find out how much wire to purchase: perimeter or area?

   _____

   b) Explain your selection in 'a'?

   _____
   _____
   _____
   _____
   _____
   _____
   _____
   _____

TASK THREE

5. Mr. Hamilton has decided to plant pak choi. He wants to use a plot with the same perimeter as **S** but a smaller area. Draw a rectangle and label it **P** to represent the plot for pak choi. Insert measurements for the length and width.

6. Complete the table below.

Figures	Perimeter (m)
C	
L	
S	
P	
G	

TASK THREE

7. Use the information in the table to construct a bar graph. Remember to label each axis and bar.

Graph showing the Perimeter of different sections of Mr. Hamilton's plot of land.

Perimeter (m)

Land usage

Task Four

In a class of fifty students a survey was carried out to determine the preference in holiday period. Fifteen students like both Christmas and summer, twenty-five like summer, thirty-five like Christmas and the others like neither of the two holidays.

1. Calculate the number of children who like summer only.

2. How many students prefer Christmas only?

TASK FOUR

3. (a) How many students like neither of the holidays?

_____
_____
_____
_____

(b) Which holiday could those children like?

_____

(c) Suggest one reason the students would prefer the holiday at (b) to the ones mentioned in the survey.

_____
_____

(d) Construct a Venn diagram to represent the information.

Task Five

ALL QUESTIONS RELATE TO THE INFORMATION GIVEN BELOW.

The length of the rectangle below is **12cm**. Its width is **6cm**.

a) Calculate the perimeter of the rectangle.

b) Calculate the surface covered (area) of the rectangle.

TASK FIVE

c) Is it possible to draw a rectangle with the same area but a smaller perimeter? _____ . If yes, **draw it. Insert the measurements and show the new perimeter.**

d) Is it possible to draw a rectangle with the same perimeter but a smaller area? _____ .
If yes, **draw it. Insert the measurements and show the new area?**

TASK FIVE

e) Is it possible to draw a rectangle with the same perimeter and a greater area? _____.

If yes, **draw it. Insert the measurements and show the new area.**

f) If a second rectangle identical to the original was placed immediately to the right of it without any gaps, what would be the new perimeter?

Task Six

Patrick, Christopher, Jhemar and Oliver each own cats. Below is a table showing how much food the cats are fed.

Cat Owners	Amount Fed
Patrick's cat	⅜ kg per day
Christopher's cat	¾ kg in two days
Jhemar's cat	1½ kg in three days
Oliver's cat	⅝ kg every 12 hours

a) Which two cats ate the same amount? _____ and _____ .

b) Explain how you arrived at your answer in 'a' above?

_____
_____
_____
_____
_____
_____
_____
_____
_____
_____

TASK SIX

c) If Chew Meow Food costs **$120** per kilogram, how much would Oliver pay to feed his cat for **5 days**?

d) Who pays **$630** to feed his cat for a week? Show how you arrived at your answer.

e) How much food is eaten by the cats in a week?

f) To feed his cat for a week (**7 days**), Patrick has to save $\frac{1}{10}$ of his monthly allowance. If the allowance is the only means by which Patrick can purchase food for his cat, how much of his allowance does he save monthly?

Task Seven

Bitter Weed Community has been experiencing an upsurge in crime and violence. Their Member of Parliament has decided to utilize an open field to facilitate a skills training centre for young adults and a multipurpose court with stands for spectators. The plan is shown below.

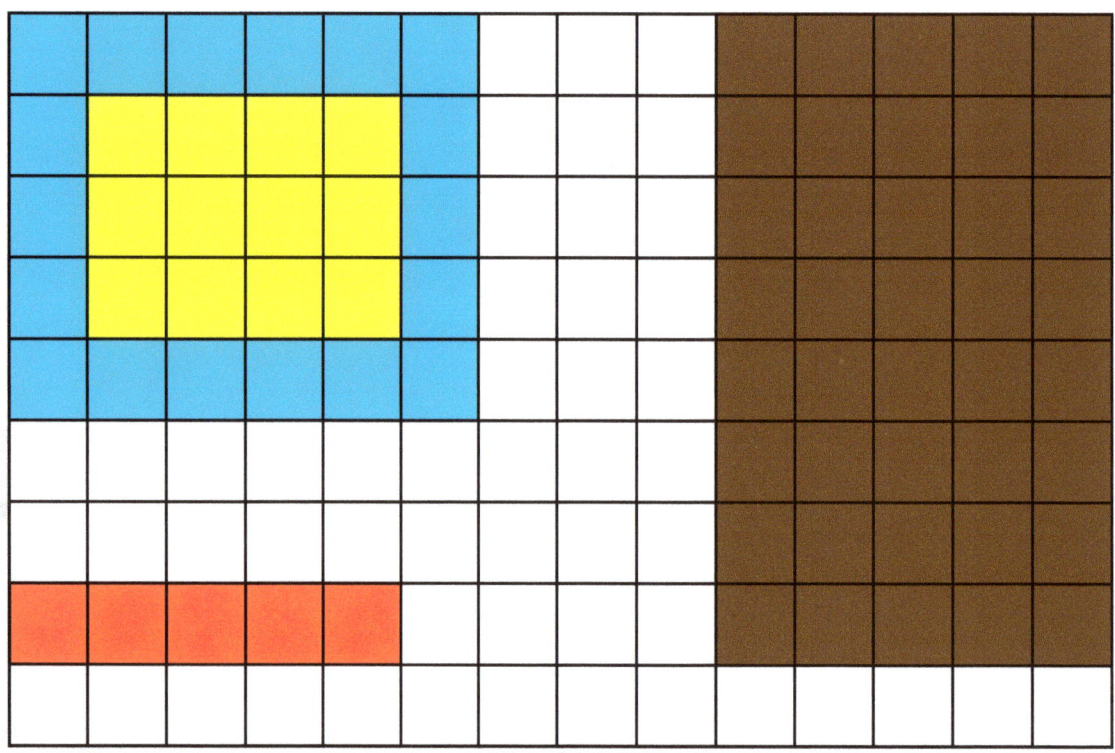

Area = 4 m²

Key
yellow: multipurpose court
blue: stands
pink: bathroom area
brown: skills training centre

TASK SEVEN

a) What is the perimeter of the skills training centre?

b) What is the area designated for the multipurpose court inclusive of the stands?

c) What is the area of the multipurpose court alone?

d) How many times can the bathroom area fit into the skills training centre?

TASK SEVEN

e) After showing the model to some parents in a community meeting, a suggestion was made to erect a playground, 48 m² for the younger children. The Member of Parliament said that he could afford it but there was no space on the land to accommodate it. He did not want the areas touching each other. There has to be space between the facilities.

Create a plan that shows all the facilities including the playground. Ensure that you label each. Use crayons to represent the different facilities.

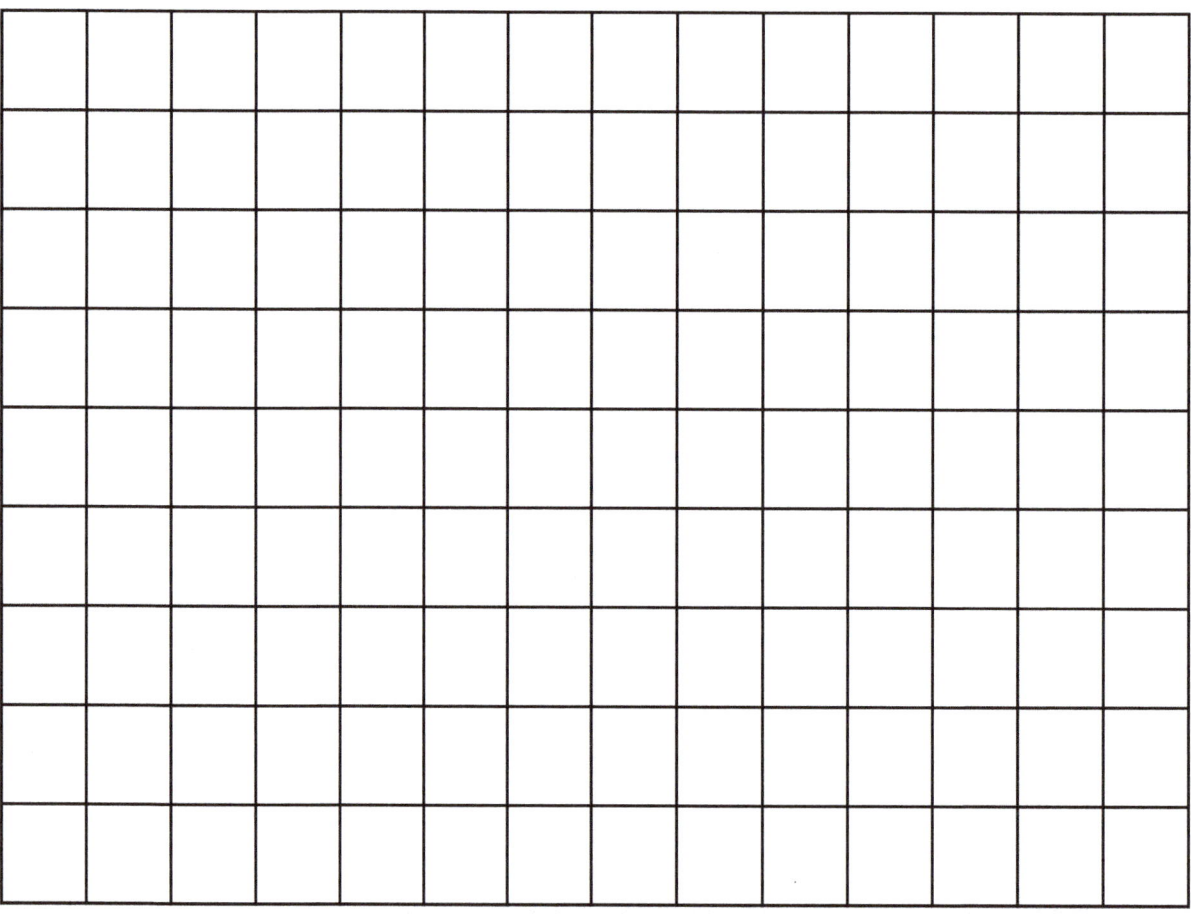

Task Eight

At an event each person was asked to record his/her age as part of a survey. The information was then presented on a stem and leaf plot.

Stem	Leaf
1	6, 6, 7, 8, 9
2	0, 2, 2, 2, 2, 3, 5, 8
3	0, 1, 1, 6, 7, 9
4	2, 4, 4, 6, 9
5	0

TASK EIGHT

Task 1

Complete the Frequency table below.

Range	Tally	Frequency
16-20		
21-25		
25-30		
30-35		
36-40		
41-45		
46-50		

Task 2

Use the information from task 1 to construct a histogram.

TASK EIGHT

TASK EIGHT

Task 3

Calculate the following from the given data.

a) Modal age

```
```

b) The range

```
```

c) The median

```
```

Task 4

Which event do you think the persons attended? Justify your suggestion in no less than three sentences.

_____
_____
_____
_____
_____
_____
_____

Task Nine

Jhemar used identical building blocks to make a solid shape. He used **6** blocks along the length, **7** blocks along the width and **8** blocks for the height. He completed the figure that was identical to a cuboid.

a) Sketch and insert measurements for the cuboid Jhemar built.

b) How many blocks in all did Jhemar use?

c) How many blocks cover the base of Jhemar's cuboid?

TASK NINE

d) Is it possible for Jhemar to use the same number of blocks to build another cuboid with a smaller area for the base? If yes, sketch the cuboid and include the number of blocks along its length, width and height.

e) If Jhemar only had half the number of blocks, could he build a cuboid with the same height as the original one? If yes, sketch the new cuboid and insert the measurements (number of blocks for each dimension).

Task Ten

Three friends, Sandra, Jaclyn and Alecia wanted to earn some money during the summer holiday. After discussing several ideas, they decided to sell 'suck suck'. They agreed that the profit earned would be divided among them based on how much each person gave as capital. Sandra contributed $400, Jaclyn $600 and Alecia $1000. They made a list of the things they needed.

Grocery Shopping

- ✓ Lime
- ✓ Syrup
- ✓ Water
- ✓ Plastic bags

TASK TEN

Sandra wanted to know in whose refrigerator the 'suck sucks' would be stored. All three girls spoke to Sandra's mother who applauded their entrepreneurial enthusiasm, but would only store the commodity at a fee. She advised them that when they were ready to sell the suck suck they would have to remove them all at once and keep them in a huge plastic basin. This would conserve energy and ensure that her electricity bill does not skyrocket. The arrangement was $500 for the light and $250 for the water each to be paid weekly. The capital will be given to Sandra's mom for safe keeping for the next year.

'Suck Suck : $50

The table shows the number of suck suck sold weekly for seven weeks.

Weeks	Amount spent on ingredients and other materials (bags)	Number of suck suck sold
Week 1	$2000	80
Week 2	$1200	100
Week 3	$1200	110
Week 4	$800	90
Week 5	$1000	100
Week 6	$1000	80
Week 7	$750	60

TASK TEN

a) How much did the children collect over the seven weeks for suck suck?

b) How much did they spend on ingredients and other materials over the seven weeks?

c) How much should Sandra's mother get at the end of the period?

d) What was the profit earned?

e) What percentage of the capital did Jaclyn contribute?

f) How much of the profit will Jaclyn get?

g) Jaclyn does not agree that Sandra's mother should get the original capital of $2000 to keep. She thinks they should put it in the bank to earn interest. Do you agree with Jaclyn?

TASK TEN

h) Explain your reason for your position.

Task Eleven

Skills: Fractions/Money

Use the information below to complete the given tasks.

- Antonio had $800. He spent $\frac{3}{8}$ of it at break time on fruits.
- Kristen bought a slice of cake. It cost the same amount as Antonio spent on fruits. She is now left with $\frac{2}{5}$ of the amount she originally had.

1. How much money does Antonio have left? Show how you arrive at your answer.

2. How much money did Kristen have before buying the slice of cake? Explain how you arrived at your response.

TASK ELEVEN

3. What percentage of her money did Kristen spend on the cake?

4. Which of the two children originally had more money?

5. Antonio says that Kristen can purchase another slice of cake using only the change she has. Do you agree? Justify the position you have taken.

Task Twelve

The Member of Parliament for South East St. Andrew decided to designate a play area to reduce the levels of crime in one community in the constituency that he represents. He spoke to some young children who told him that they wanted a sandbox, monkey bar, trampoline, see-saw, swing and slide. The youths desired a football field, netball court and an area for volleyball.

The M.P. explained that he could only take on two of the suggestions with the space **40m** by **30m**. He has shared the plan that he had in mind with the community.

The height of the sandbox is **4m**

Part 1

a) What length of fencing would be required for the play area?

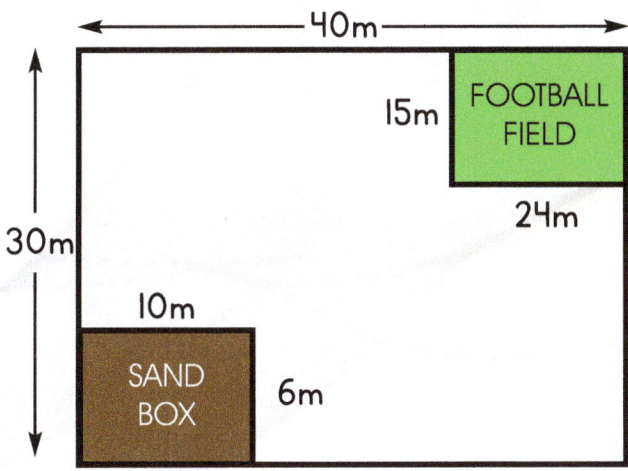

TASK TWELVE

b) How much surface does the football field cover?

c) Express the width of the sandbox in centimetres.

d) How much surface is still available for the other suggested projects?

e) How many times can the surface covered by the sandbox be taken from the area of the playground?
_____
_____
_____

Part 2

a) One bag of sand holds 15m³ and costs $850. How many bags would be needed to half fill the sandbox?
_____
_____

TASK TWELVE

b) Grass is sold at **$275** per **m²** and is needed to cover the football field. How much money would be needed to execute the task?

c) The M.P. loves the idea of the sandbox. He plans to purchase a dozen buckets at **$250** each, the same number of shovels at **$150** each, 6 plastic balls at **$80** each and 10 plastic rakes at **$200** for **2**.

A budget is a plan showing how much money is available (income) and how it will be spent (expenditure).

Complete the budget sheet below.

Budget for Community Project

Income		Expenditure	
Capital	$250,000	Cost of land	$150,000
		Wood for sandbox	$ 3,000
		Sand	$ _____
		Grass for the field	$ _____
		Buckets	$ _____
		Shovels	$ _____
		Balls	$ _____
		Rakes	$ _____
		TOTAL	_____

d. Does the M.P. have enough money? Yes or no. If no, how much more does he need?

_____

_____

Task Thirteen

Your school's auditorium has a length of **30m** and a width of **18m**. This is where devotion is held daily. The principal wants to designate a 'naughty corner' area for those who display irreverent behaviour during devotion.

Use the information to respond to the two parts in this performance task.

Part 1

a) The length of the naughty corner will be one fifth of the length of the auditorium and the width will be one-third of the width of the auditorium. How much space will be available for those who are NOT IRREVERENT?

b) If a space of **2m²** can comfortably fit 6 students in a standing position, what is the maximum number of students that can be sent to stand in the 'naughty corner' during devotion?

TASK THIRTEEN

c) The principal has informed the student body that the 'naughty corner' will be painted black. If one can of paint can cover $15m^2$ of the floor, would 2 cans be enough? Justify your answer.

d) Painter Dean charges $120 for m^2. How much will it cost to paint the auditorium floor excluding the 'naughty corner'?

e) The entire auditorium is bordered with red ribbon. What length of ribbon was used?

f) You were asked to make a scale drawing of the auditorium. You decided to use the scale **4cm: 3m**. What measurement must be used on the drawing to show

   i) the width of the auditorium?

   ii) the length of the auditorium?

   iii) What will be the area of the model of the auditorium that was drawn by scale?

TASK THIRTEEN

iv) Represent the auditorium including the 'naughty corner'. Each small square represents $9m^2$.

Task Fourteen

The diagram below shows how a section of a school yard is utilized.

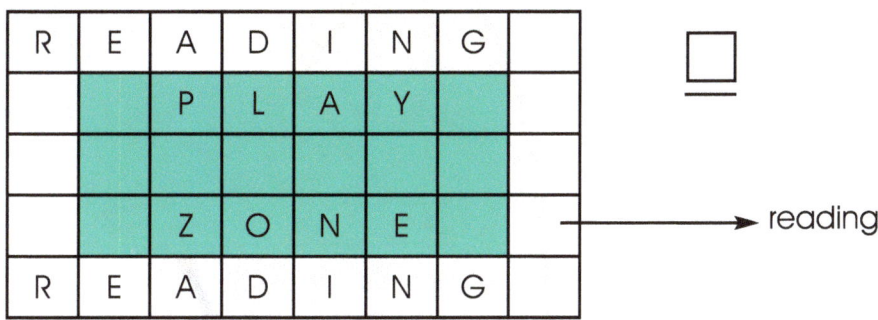

Part A

1) What is the area of the play zone field?

___
___
___

2) What is the area of the section designated for reading?

___
___
___

At a sports committee meeting they decided to grass the play zone; also, they plan to enclose it with sound proof plastic to reduce the level of noise which disturbs the students who read. Grass is sold at $250 per m^2 and the sound proof plastic is sold at $625 per metre. The bursar of the school has announced that there is sixty three thousand dollars allocated for this proposed project.

TASK FOURTEEN

3) Which of the proposed tasks will be more costly? Use mathematics to explain/justify your response.

4) Can the budget cover the plans of the committee? Give a clear reason for your answer.

TASK FOURTEEN

Part B

5) Some students lost interest in reading and the principal has decided to increase the play zone by one-third of its current size. No change will be made to the reading area. Represent the new plan. Remember to label the areas.

6) What is the length of the new play zone? _____
_____
_____
_____

7) What is the new width of the play zone? _____
_____
_____
_____

Task Fifteen

Mrs. Blair bought a house but it needs to be fenced. She has to consider the cost of labour in addition to the cost of blocks, cement, steel and sand. She needs **300 (8 inch)** blocks, **3** yards of sand, **2** yards of gravel, **12** lengths of steel and nine bags of cement. She already has enough binding wire to make columns with the steel. She was told that there are three establishments that offer great deals.

Smart Buy Construction

100 blocks = $9,000
Cement: $1,100
Sand: $2,200
Gravel: $26,325
Steel: $650 per length

Adrian's Hardware

100 blocks = $8,500
Cement: $1,200
Sand: $2,200
Gravel: $22,550
Steel: $800 per length

Buildings Are Us

100 blocks = $8,800
Cement: $1,050
Sand: $2,200
Gravel: $23,250
Steel: $900 per length

Part 1

1) How much more would it cost Mrs. Blair to purchase the gravel from Smart Buy Construction instead of Adrian's Hardware?

_____
_____

TASK FIFTEEN

2) Which of the three establishments is providing the most affordable price? Show your working and an explanation.

_____
_____
_____
_____

3) If Mrs. Blair decides to purchase the items from the different establishments, where should she buy each?

_____
_____
_____
_____

Items	Smart Buy Construction	Adrian's Hardware	Buildings Are Us
Sand			
Gravel			
Steel			
Cement			
Block			

Part 2

a) Mr. Bonner placed **5** blocks beside each other without gaps along the length of a space and **3** blocks along the width of the same space to form a rectangle.

What is the area of the surface enclosed by the blocks?

_____

TASK FIFTEEN

b) Mr. Bonner decides to use more blocks to fill in the rectangle making a cuboid. How many blocks would Mr. Bonner use in total to construct a cuboid with height of 9 inches?

c) Could Mr. Bonner use the same number of blocks used in 4b, to model another cuboid but with different dimensions? Yes or no. If yes, explain how he could do it.

Section 2 - Language Arts

Skills

Language Arts Performance Task requires a particular set of skills directly related to comprehension. Before you begin to practise the activities in this section, spend some time familiarizing yourself with the following terms:

1. **Analyse:** to examine in detail in order to explain and interpret it. It is like taking a whole and breaking it into parts.

2. **Compare:** Note the ways in which the given sources are similar.

3. **Contrast:** Note the ways in which sources are different.

4. **Describe:** to give details about a subject.

5. **Discuss:** Write about a topic in detail ensuring that different ideas or issues related to the topic are highlighted and examined.

6. **Evaluate:** This means to assess a subject matter. Tell the positives and negatives about a subject in order to make a judgement about it.

7. **Explain:** to make something clear by describing it in detail and relating relevant facts.

8. **Formulate:** to create, compose, plan, or construct.

SKILLS

9. **Infer:** to draw a conclusion from evidence and reasoning, not from what is stated. It is more like reading between the lines.

10. **Predict:** to make an informed guess about what will happen next, based on the content of what is read.

11. **Summarize:** to give a brief account of an event or text by writing the main points.

12. **Support:** to provide evidence as proof for taking a particular stance or position.

13. **Trace:** Find or describe the origin or development of something.

14. **Synthesise:** To combine different parts into one whole.

Context Clues

Have you ever read a book and came across unfamiliar words? Did you lose interest? Don't worry! There is no need to panic; use context clues.

Context clues are words, phrases or sentences given by the author to help the reader unlock the meaning of unfamiliar words. The writer may use one of the following:

- **synonym/restatement**
- **an antonym/contrast**
- **an example**
- **an explanation/definition.**

Contrast/Antonym: Patrick is **garrulous**, but his younger brother Sean is extremely **quiet**.

Synonym/Restatement: Nia was **remorseful** or **sorry** for the behaviour she displayed in the presence of her parents.

Explanation/Definition: The **mediator**, the **one who was hired to settle the dispute**, is not a friend or relative of the conflicting parties.

Example: Luminous objects like **stars, fireflies** and **light bulbs**, are primary sources of light.

Main Idea

The main idea of a paragraph is what the paragraph is chiefly about. It may be stated or implied (suggested). The main idea is usually, but not always, the first sentence of the paragraph. It may be found in the middle or at the end of the paragraph.

CONTEXT CLUES

The main idea can be easily identified if you pay close attention to the supporting sentences. These sentences present details about the main idea. The supporting sentences help the reader to determine the writer's purpose.

Sequencing

When we sequence, we place related events in a logical order. This makes the text easier to understand. Look out for signal words such as **first, next, then, finally, afterwards** to aid in ordering events.

Facts and Opinions

A **fact** is a statement that can be proven to be true. It can be about people, places or things.

Example: Teachers are not paid as well as doctors.

An **opinion** is a statement that CANNOT be proven to be exclusively true. It is a personal feeling, idea or thought about a subject.

Example: Male teachers are better at their jobs than female teachers.

Making Inference

To infer means to come to a reasonable or logical conclusion made solely on evidence. This is one of the most important comprehension skills. You have to use facts or details given to help you figure out what is NOT stated. You have to develop the skill of reading between and beneath the lines of the text.

Cause and Effect

This is a relationship between the 'reason for something happening' and the 'impact it has' on something.

CONTEXT CLUES

Cause tells why or gives the reason for an event, occurrence or incident, while the effect tells the result or consequence of the act or the cause.

Example: The teacher was summoned to the office because she had punished the student.

Cause: a student was punished.

Effect: the teacher was called to the office.

The students who excelled in the tests were awarded with cash and certificates.

Cause: The students excelled in the test.

Effect: They were awarded cash and certificates.

Comparing and Contrasting

As a reader you must be able to see similarities and differences between people, places, things, events, situations, ideas, opinions and point of views. To compare means to look for similarities between ideas. Comparison refers to the differences between ideas.

Predicting Outcomes

To predict is to foretell what you believe will happen. A prediction is not based solely on opinion, but on the basis of observation, past events, trends or simply your knowledge. When you read a title of a story or you see the picture on the cover does that give you a hint at what the story will be about? When the thunder rolls and the lightning flashes across a dark sky, I am sure you don't predict that it will be a fair day to go on a picnic. Predictions are made based on information that you will read in the text.

CONTEXT CLUES

Summarizing

A summary is a brief version of a written piece. Your summary must be shorter than the original piece. First, select the main ideas and express them in your own words without changing the original idea to show that you understand what you read. Leave out examples, and explanations. Do not add new information as this would no longer be a summary. Book reports are good examples of summaries.

Task One

Carefully read each source before attempting the tasks. The responses should be based only on the information presented.

Source A

Jamaica Independence At Last

The British flag that reigned over us for over 300 years,
Finally breathed its last little breath before midnight on August 5, 1962
No longer were we a nation without our own identity

At exactly 30 minutes before midnight
Our black, green and gold stood tall
Pride and tears filled the faces of those who were present
Yes, it all happened at our National Stadium
I wasn't there, but that's what I hear

Can you imagine the shouts of joy, the fireworks, the celebration?
That was the birth of a nation…. My Jamaica!!!

Can you imagine how di people dem glad bag burs'
When dem hear seh Bustamante was going to be Prime Minista?
Our own Jamaican born, son of the soil
Black like we, talk like we, look like we

TASK ONE

Mi can imagine how di people dem crowd roun
Fi listen di news on Mas Joe lickle radio in dem community
Den di big day came, when everybody from near an far

Bundle up inna di National Stadium
Ready fi sing, crow or talk wi National Anthem.
The flag was flown with pride, it was the beginning of something new

All di talk bout independence was finally coming true
Independence now meant we were responsible for our own affairs
We could elect our own government and people fi represent wi
Independence meant we had our own Jamaican currency
Our own symbols, our own constitution
Yes, ours, not theirs, ours!!

Source B

God save our gracious Queen! Long live our noble Queen! God save the Queen! Send her victorious, Happy and glorious, Long to reign over us: God save the Queen! O Lord our God arise, Scatter her enemies, And make them fall: Confound their politics, Frustrate their knavish tricks, On Thee our hopes we fix: God save us all.	Eternal Father bless our land Guard us with thy mighty hand Keep us free from evil powers Be our light through countless hours To our leaders, Great Defender Grant true wisdom from above Justice, truth be ours forever Jamaica, Land we love Jamaica, Jamaica Jamaica, Land we love. Teach us true respect for all Stir response to duty's call Strengthen us the weak to cherish Give us vision lest we perish Knowledge send us, Heavenly Father Grant true wisdom from above Justice, truth be ours forever Jamaica, Land we love Jamaica, Jamaica Jamaica, Land we love.

TASK ONE

TASK ONE

Source C

On August 6, 1962, Jamaica became an independent country. For the first time Jamaicans were fully responsible for ruling themselves. For 300 years the British flag was Jamaica's flag too because Jamaica was a part of the British Empire. The Empire was England and all the countries it owned and ruled.

Before independence, Jamaicans sang the anthem of England. The words in this anthem say nothing specific about Jamaica. The anthem only mentions the queen and the empire. When the country became independent in 1962, it stopped using the British flag. We had our own anthem and our own flag. Our flag was designed by the House of Representatives in May, 1962. It is rectangular in shape with a diagonal cross which divides into four triangles. Three colours are on the flag and each has its own meaning.

TASK ONE

Activity 1

a) Give two comparisons between source A and C. (2 marks)

_____
_____
_____
_____
_____

b) Give one contrast between source C and A. (1 mark)

_____
_____
_____
_____
_____
_____

c) According to Source A, what did independence mean to Jamaica?

(2 marks)

_____
_____
_____
_____
_____

d) What is the main difference between the two anthems presented in source B?

(2 marks)

_____
_____
_____
_____
_____

TASK ONE

e) Write the first line of the anthem that would have been used prior to August, 1962.

(1 mark)

_____
_____
_____

Activity 2

Read each statement and indicate whether you should agree or disagree based on the information in the sources.

(6 marks: 1 each)

Statements	Source A	Source B	Source C	None of the sources
The source is written in stanzas.				
Lyrics to Britain's national anthem is in this source.				
The colours of Jamaica's flag can be found in this source.				
The writer of the national anthem of Jamaica is in this source.				
The meaning of the colours on the flag is shared in this source.				
This tells where the independence was hosted.				

Activity 3

TASK ONE

For each statement given, place a tick to indicate the source it relates to.

(6 marks: 1 each)

Statements	Source A	Source B	Source C	None of the sources
The source is written in stanzas.				
Lyrics to Britain's national anthem is in this source.				
The colours of Jamaica's flag can be found in this source.				
The writer of the national anthem of Jamaica is in this source.				
The meaning of the colours on the flag is shared in this source.				
This tells where the independence was hosted.				

Task Two

Source 1

Everybady wat a gwan?
Run come, run come,
Tings a gwan.
Dem seh all a wi a go vote
Poor man, beggarman, but no tief
Dem seh a fi wi time now
Fi jump an shout,
Universal Adult Suffrage

Everybady
Teacha, docta, lawya, preacha
Dung to di jailhouse keepa
A fi wi time now
Run come, run come,
Tings a gwan,
Universal Adult Suffrage

Missa Matalon, Missa Azan
An all di businessman dem
Come join us
Wi a celebrate di rite
Di rite fi vote
Dem call it
Universal Adult Suffrage.
A dis a gwan

Adrian Mandara

TASK TWO

Source 2

After the riots in 1938, the English government sent a delegation (special group of people) to Jamaica to find out why the people were so angry. Among their recommendations, this team, called the **Moyne Commission**, told the British government that it would be a good thing if more Jamaicans had the right to vote. They also said that Jamaicans of all classes and colour should be allowed to be part of the government. The British government agreed. In 1944, a law was passed that gave the right to vote to all Jamaicans over 21 years. At that time 21 years was the legal adult age. Thirty-two years later, the age was lowered to 18 years. The right to vote is called suffrage. The right or opportunity for all adults to vote is known as universal adult suffrage.

Source 3

Grandma Dell: Jonathan, aren't you going to cast your vote this election?

Jonathan: No

Grandma Dell: What! Do you understand the privilege you have to be able to vote?

Jonathan: Marking an X on a paper and dipping your index finger in a bottle with ink doesn't seem like much of an opportunity to me, Grandma.

Grandma Dell: Well, maybe if you knew the history of voting, you would look at it differently. Before 1944, less than 50,000 Jamaicans were able to vote. Jamaica was under the British rule at that time, so elections were held to elect the Crown Colony government. The right to vote depended on the following: the amount of land someone owned, the ability to pay taxes and the ability to read.

TASK TWO

Jonathan: This would be mainly Europeans and their descendants. What about the Asian immigrants?

Grandma Dell: They were not allowed unless they met the criteria I shared earlier. Only after 1944 were all people, regardless of their ancestors or ethnicity, able to vote.

Jonathan: Thanks for all that information. I will be using my vote to decide who should take care of the country's business.

Grandma Dell: That's better! The only reason you shouldn't vote is if you are serving a prison sentence or if you are mentally ill. I pray to God that you will never be in either situation.

TASK TWO

Activity 1

In source 3, a criterion is given that people would have to meet in order to vote. Suggest one other possible criterion that existed but was not mentioned in the source.

(2 marks)

_____
_____
_____
_____
_____
_____
_____
_____
_____

TASK TWO

Activity 2

Insert the Source that applies to each statement. (8 marks)

a) The source that gives a definition of universal adult suffrage.
_____

b) The source that is not written in standard Jamaican English.
_____

c) The source that includes the specific groups of people who could vote.
_____

d) The source that tells the group of people who are not allowed to vote.
_____

e) Source that could be taken from a textbook or newspaper article.
_____

f) Source that is written in stanzas.
_____

g) Source that is called a dialogue.
_____

h) The source that could be used to determine the year in which the age for voting was lowered to 18. _____
_____

Activity 3

TASK TWO

a) From which ethnic group are Missa Issa and Missa Hanna most likely from?
(1 mark)

_____
_____
_____

b) In which year was the age for voting lowered? (1 mark)

_____

c) Which source do you think gave more details? (1 mark)

_____
_____

d) Give three similarities between sources 2 and 3. (3 marks)

_____
_____
_____
_____

e) Give one difference between sources 2 and 3. (1 mark)

_____
_____
_____

f) If you were to conduct a small research on Universal Adult Suffrage and were presented with the three sources above but could only use two, which source would you exclude and why? (3 marks)

_____
_____
_____

Task Three

Source 1

Alexander Bustamante, born William Clarke in the parish of Hanover in 1884, became a national hero because of his struggles for self government. He was concerned about the wages and workingconditions of the workers in Jamaica. He stood up for the rights of the workers when they went on strike. This led to his arrest. His cousin, Norman Manley bailed him.

Alexander organized workers to form the Bustamante Industrial Trade Union (BITU) in 1938. He also started the Jamaica Labour Party (JLP) in 1943. He became Chief Minister and later, Prime Minister when we gained Independence. He was actively involved in leading Jamaica to be an independent nation in 1962. He died in 1977.

Norman Manley was born in Roxborough, Manchester in 1893. He became a national hero because of struggles for self government. He was concerned for the rioting of the workers, and after holding meetings with workers and their employers, he got them to end the rioting. Using his skills as a lawyer, he persuaded the governor to release his cousin, Alexander Bustamante from jail.

Norman was instrumental in starting the following organizations: Jamaica Banana Producers Association, Social Development Commission, People's National Party (1938) and National Workers' Union.

TASK THREE

In 1944, Norman Manley was able to convince the British Government to give all adults the right to vote. These Jamaicans included the poor Blacks. This right was known as the Universal Adult Suffrage.

Manley served as Chief Minister of Jamaica between 1955 and 1959 and as Premier between 1959 and 1962. He, along with Alexander Bustamante led Jamaica into Independence in 1962. He died in 1969.

Source 2

Questions	Norman Manley	Alexander Bustamante
Who were their parents?	Margaret Ann Shearer and Thomas Manley	Mary Wilson and Robert Clarke
Where did they go to school?	Beckford and Smith Secondary School (now St. Jago High) Jamaica College University of Oxford	Cocoon and Dalmalley Elementary School
Did they have siblings?	Sisters: Vera and Murial Brother: Roy	Sisters: Ida, Louise, Daisy, Maud, Iris Brother: Herbert
Who did they marry?	Edna Swithenbank	Gladys Longbridge
Do they have children?	Sons - Michael and Douglas	None

TASK THREE

Source 3

- Norman Manley Law School
- Norman Manley High School
- Norman Manley Boulevard
- Norman Manley International Airport

- Bustamante Children's Hospital
- Bustamante High School
- Bustamante Highway
- Port Bustamante

Activity 1

Construct a six point timeline showing events and dates in the life of Norman Manley. His birth and death must be included. **(6 marks)**

TASK THREE

Activity 2

a) From the information given, list three similarities between Norman Manley and Alexander Bustamante. (3 marks)

_____
_____
_____
_____
_____
_____

b) Give one difference between the two nation builders. (1 mark)

_____
_____
_____
_____

Activity 3

Tick the source that would provide the information in each statement. (4 marks)

STATEMENTS	SOURCE 1	SOURCE 2	SOURCE 3
a) The source that provides information on ways in which the country honoured the heroes.			
b) The source that gives information about the heroes' personal life.			
c) Without this source, you cannot calculate the age of death of the heroes.			
d) If you were required to write a report on the life of one of the heroes, this source would be best.			

TASK THREE

Read each statement and indicate whether or not it is supported or not. (4 marks)

Statements	Supported	Not Supported
a) Manley spent more time being formerly educated than Bustamante.		
b) Alexander Bustamante had six siblings.		
c) Norman Manley has more places named in his honour than Alexander Bustamante.		
d) The heroes are honoured by having their image on coins.		

In your opinion, which of the nation builders named in the sources contributed more to Jamaica? Justify your choice. (2 marks)

_____
_____
_____
_____
_____
_____
_____
_____
_____
_____
_____
_____
_____
_____
_____

Task Four

Source 1

Some influences of the ethnic groups on Caribbean culture

Ethnic Group	Language or words	Food	Dress	Religion	Buildings	Entertainment
English	English	Steak, Porridge, Pies, Flour products	Skirts, pants, shirts, blouses, jackets, ties	Christianity (eg Anglican, Presbyterian)	Church buildings	Cricket and football
Africans	Nyam Brawta Pickney		Dashiki head ties, braids	Pukkumina Shango	-	Anancy stories and Jonkunnu

TASK FOUR

Source 2

Africans were taken from their villages in West Africa by force and brought to the Caribbean to work on sugar plantations as slaves. The Africans brought to the Caribbean as slaves belonged to different ethnic groups: Mandingoes, Fanti, Ashant, Iboes, Whydas and Pawpas.

The slaves did all the work on the sugar plantations and in the great houses. They were divided into two groups: House and field slaves. House slaves washed, cooked, cleaned and served the planters and their families. They were generally women and girls. Both women and men worked as field slaves.

Field slaves carried out a number of tasks: they were the labour force on the plantations; planted, weeded and cut the canes; tested the sugar to see if it was boiled; cultivated food for the plantations; worked as carpenters, repairing furniture, carts and the sugar mills; sometimes they worked as blacksmiths, repairing tools and putting shoes on horses.

The English who came to the Caribbean brought their language, religious beliefs, customs, food, dress and social life. They introduced systems of government that still exist in the Caribbean. Games like dominoes and cricket are known in Jamaica because of them. It was the English who divided the island into parishes and counties. They ruled over the slaves and were very harsh in order to gain wealth. Certainly they were vexed when the system of slavery was abolished.

TASK FOUR

1. Compare the contribution made by both groups to the Jamaican society.

   _____
   _____
   _____
   _____
   _____
   _____
   _____
   _____
   _____
   _____

2. Which group contributed more to the Jamaican society?
   Justify your choice in no less than three sentences.

   _____
   _____
   _____
   _____
   _____
   _____
   _____
   _____
   _____

3. Pretend that you were an African during the period of slavery in Jamaica. Write a paragraph describing a typical day as **either** a field slave or a house slave. Give your response an appropriate title.

   _____
   _____
   _____
   _____
   _____
   _____
   _____
   _____

TASK FOUR

Task Five

Read the information in the following sources.

Source A

> Di Inglish dem bring in bout 260 pretty hair people today: man woman an pickney. Dem must tired. Dem did haffi walk from the train station to di plantation. Di planta dem gi dem one suit a clothes, work tools and cooking utensils. How so much a dem ago hol inna di likkle room? Mi think twenty a to much!
>
> Mi nuh think wi ago get along especially if dem pay dem more dan me and my people. Hope dem can chop di cane and stay long inna di sun like wi.

TASK FIVE

Source B

During the period 1845 to 1921 36 000 East Indians, mainly of the Hindu faith, were brought to Jamaica to work as indentured labourers on the sugar plantations. They were paid less than ex-slaves and were therefore at the bottom of the society. In India, under the Caste system, light skin was valued over dark skin. Based on this aspect of their culture, The Indians looked down on the ex-slaves. This was a recipe for conflict between the two groups in the initial stages of their interactions.

TASK FIVE

Source C

> **November 18, 1838**
>
> Today, I received 200 indentured labourers. They were tired and hungry but appeared to be healthy. I anticipate that they will work hard and be a success as those in Mauritius. It cost a lot of money to get them here so they better be prepared to work hard. Since I will have to supply them weekly with food (rice, flour, peas, seasoning, fish or goat), I will have to reduce the initial amount agreed upon as their weekly wages.

Task 1

Read each statement carefully and tick whether you agree or disagree with it.

Statements	Agree	Disagree
a) Source A is most likely taken from a journal.		
b) Source C is possibly from a diary.		
c) Source B could have been taken from a textbook or a newspaper.		
d) Source B speaks to the religious beliefs of the people who came.		
e) All three sources were written by the same person.		

TASK FIVE

Task 2

a) Whom do you think wrote source A? Suggest a reason for your response.
_____
_____
_____
_____

b) What is the main idea of Source B?
_____
_____
_____
_____

c) What are two similarities between sources A and B?
_____
_____
_____
_____

d) Whom do you think wrote source A? Which group of people could the writer be referring to as having 'pretty hair'?
_____
_____
_____
_____

Task 3

Source **A** is written in Jamaican Creole (JC). Rewrite it in Standard Jamaican English (SJE).

_____
_____
_____
_____
_____
_____
_____
_____
_____
_____
_____
_____
_____
_____
_____
_____
_____
_____
_____
_____

Task 4

Pretend that you are an Indentured East Indian. In your note books, write a letter to a family member back home in India describing your experience on the plantation.

Task Six

Source 1

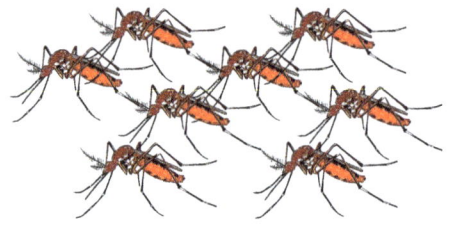

Dengue is an infection caused by a virus spread by the bite of an infected Aedes mosquito. There are four Dengue Types: 1, 2, 3 and 4. You can only be infected with each 'type' once in your lifetime. When infected with a dengue virus you may develop one of the following: Dengue Fever or Dengue Haemorrhagic Fever. Dengue Haemorrhagic Fever is the more severe form of Dengue. Children, as well as persons who have had Dengue before, are more likely to get Dengue Haemorrhagic Fever.

Although it is a severe illness and affects both children and adults, Dengue Fever rarely causes death. Some common symptoms include a sudden start of high fever accompanied by some or all of the following: severe headache, pain behind eyes, muscle pains, bone or joint pains, skin rash, vomiting or a feeling that you want to vomit. If you experience these symptoms – if you feel like you have Dengue Fever, visit your doctor or the nearest health clinic. Get plenty of rest; drink lots of fluid; use only paracetamol pain killers, as other pain killers may increase the risk of internal bleeding.

Source 2

Dengue Haemorrhagic Fever is the form of dengue which often causes death. Persons with this form of dengue may have all the symptoms of Dengue Fever in addition to

- Fainting
- Difficulty breathing
- Pale, cold, clammy skin
- Bleeding from the nose, mouth and/or gums
- Severe and continuous stomach pain
- Skin bruising
- Frequent vomiting with or without blood

These complications usually start after the fever goes down. In severe cases, patients go into 'shock' called Dengue Shock Syndrome. If you are displaying symptoms and signs of Dengue Haemorrhagic Fever, go to the nearest hospital.

Source 3

Stop Aedes mosquito breeding! Look for anything water can settle in and cover it, keep it dry, clean it regularly, fill it with soil, punch holes in it, recycle or dispose of it. Protect yourself from being bitten by mosquitoes! Use insect repellent containing deet, use mosquito nets, use mosquito destroyers, and put screens on windows and doors.

TASK SIX

Task 1

What is the purpose of all the sources?

_____
_____
_____
_____

Contrast Dengue fever and Dengue Haemorrhagic Fever.

_____
_____
_____
_____
_____
_____
_____
_____
_____

Task 2

Source 1 has approximately 200 words. Summarise it in no more than fifty (50) words.

_____
_____
_____
_____
_____
_____
_____
_____
_____
_____

Task 3

Use the information in the sources to formulate a poster to share with a group of Grade 6 students.

Task Seven

Source 1

Courtney Andrew Walsh aka "Mark" or "Cuddy" was born on the 30th of October 1962. The Melbourne Cricket club was the starting point of this legend. Born on the southern wall at Melbourne, Courtney grew up on cricket, hearing the sound of bat hitting ball, evening after evening.

During his high school years he attended Excelsior High school. There Courtney specialized in Accounts and Commerce; however, he was most passionate about cricket. Courtney joined the Sunlight Cup Cricket team at Excelsior where he made local history as the only school boy to capture all 10 wickets in an inning in a match against Camperdown High.

Walsh was selected as a member of the Jamaica youth team in 1983 where he contributed towards the team's victories. Two clubs sought to have his services.

TASK SEVEN

Courtney was a member of The West Indies Cricket team for 18 years starting on his journey to success in 1984 – 85 when he had his test debut against Australia at Perth. Courtney took his first wicket.

A decade and a half later, with centuries of wickets taken and much experience, on March 27, 2000, Courtney Walsh achieved a major milestone by reaching the 500 test wicket mark. This was achieved against South Africa in Port of Spain. His 519th and last wicket came when he bowled A. Donald for 10 runs in the match West Indies played against South Africa at Kingston in 2000- 01 thus setting the world record for the most test wickets taken. It was on this day, April 23rd, 2001 that Courtney Walsh announced his retirement from international cricket.

Courtney Walsh mastered the art of bowling but unfortunately not batting. Walsh now holds the record for the highest number of test ducks (43) whenever he bats. The 'energizer bunny', 'workhorse', 'war horse', 'old soldier', 'veteran', 'iron man' – names which acknowledge the reliability, stamina, perseverance and sheer will that have kept him playing long past the average life of a fast bowler.

Source: National Library of Jamaica (www.nlj.gov.jm)

TASK SEVEN

Source 2

Courtney Walsh has received several awards for his great achievements. Some of which are listed below.

- 131 test matches, the most by any West Indian.

- In 1987 – one of the Wisden's five cricketers of the year for 1986.

- 1999 – Carreras Sportsman for 1998.

- 11th of March 1999 – Ambassador at large and special representative of the Government of Jamaica by the then Prime Minister P.J. Patterson. Courtney also received the keys to the city of Kingston, along with a citation and a copy granting him his keys.

- October 11th, 2001 – the University of West Indies Guild of Graduates prestigious Pelican Award under the theme, "Humanity, Humility and Excellence.

- The Chaconia Medal (gold), which is the second highest honour in Trinidad and Tobago.

- March 2001 – the Barbadian Honour, the Gold Crown of Merit during the third Cable and Wireless Test in Bridgetown presented by Sir Clifford Husbands (Barbadian Governor General).

- 2001 – University of the West Indies Guild of Graduates prestigious Pelican Award.

TASK SEVEN

- June 20th, 2005 – road where Melbourne Cricket Club is located was renamed 'Courtney Walsh Drive', which was previously known as Derrymore Road.

- 1993 – The Order of Distinction Commander Class (CD) and the Order of Jamaica (OJ), Jamaica's 3rd highest National Honour.

- Walsh has an award named after him consisting of a trophy and $500,000, which will be presented to athletes who have represented Jamaica in sports and who have reflected high performance, the qualities of National pride, fine conduct on and off the field and grit and determination.

Source: National Library of Jamaica (www.nlj.gov.jm)
Source: https://nlj.gov.jm/biographies/courtney-walsh-1962/

TASK SEVEN

Source 3

The University of the West Indies recognised Jamaican, Christopher Gayle, cricket legend, for his contribution to the "region's game".

Christopher Gayle, who attended Excelsior High school, credits the Lucas Cricket Club for his current status. Gayle received his plaque that commemorated the occasion. Over the years he has played for several teams locally and internationally: Bangalore, Somerset, St Kitts and Nevis Patriots, Stanford Superstars, Sydney Thunder, Vancouver Knights, Western Australia, and Worcestershire.

The left-handed batsman's tribute was read by the dean of the Faculty of Sports at The UWI, Dr Akshai Mansingh, while the plaque was presented by the Vice Chancellor Professor Hilary Beckles, who is a passionate cricket fan and cricket historian.

A smiling Gayle said: "I want to thank The University of the West Indies, Professor Beckles and the entire team. It's good to be recognised when you have achieved the outstanding during your career. I am very thankful and hopefully

TASK SEVEN

I will set more standards, set more records, before I actually depart from the game.

Members of the Chris Gayle cricket academy were on hand to see the man himself receive the award, and Gayle is certain that they would have been inspired by the moment.

Source: Source: Adapted from The Jamaica Observer, July 21, 2016.

TASK SEVEN

Task 1

Read each statement and based on the sources, evaluate them as being true or false.

Statements	False	Fact	Opinion
Both athletes attended Calabar High School.			
Walsh is better at cricket than Gayle.			
Both athletes broke records in track and field.			
Walsh has been honoured by countries other than his own.			
Gayle inspires more young people than Walsh.			

Task 2

Write **three** similarities between Chris Gayle and Courtney Walsh.

_____
_____
_____
_____
_____
_____
_____
_____
_____
_____
_____

Task 3

Pretend that source I is one chapter of a book about Jamaican athletes. You were asked to write a report on the chapter. It is to be no more than eighty (words). You must ensure that proper grammar and punctuation are primary and that it is written in your own words. Write the report on the lines provided.

_____
_____
_____
_____
_____
_____
_____
_____
_____
_____
_____
_____
_____
_____
_____
_____
_____
_____
_____
_____
_____
_____
_____
_____
_____

Task Eight

Source 1

Climate change is the rise in average surface temperatures on Earth, mostly due to the burning of fossil fuels. Scientists believe that climate change is due primarily to the human use of fossil fuels, which releases carbon dioxide and other greenhouse gases into the air. The gases trap heat within the atmosphere, which can have a range of effects on ecosystems, including rising sea levels, severe weather events, and droughts that make the land at risk to wildfires.

The primary cause of climate change is the burning of fossil fuels, such as oil and coal, which emit greenhouse gases into the atmosphere - mainly carbon dioxide. Other human activities, such as agriculture and deforestation, also contribute to the increase of greenhouse gases that cause climate change.

While some quantities of these gases occur naturally and are a critical part of Earth's temperature control system, the atmospheric concentration of carbon dioxide is at a level that is not required.

Rising sea levels due to the melting of the polar ice caps (again, caused by global warming) contribute to greater storm damage; warming ocean temperatures are associated with stronger and more frequent storms; additional rainfall, particularly during severe weather events, leads to flooding and other damage; an increase in the incidence and severity of wildfires threatens habitats, homes and lives; and heat waves contribute to human deaths and other consequences.

Source 2

A key step towards preventing global warming is to conserve energy. The vast majority of energy that we consume is produced from the burning of fossil fuels such as coal, oil, and gas. During this process, greenhouse gases are released into the atmosphere – gases that contribute to the artificial warming of our planet. By conserving energy, we will reduce the levels of fossil fuels that we burn, therefore reducing the level of greenhouse gases released into the atmosphere. We can conserve energy in our everyday life. Since vehicles consume much fuel, we can make some changes in the way we commute: walk or ride a bicycle when making short journeys and practise carpooling. Use renewable sources of energy: solar, wind, geothermal, hydroelectric power. Practise the three R's: reuse, reduce and recycle. We can also limit the number of children per family because an increase in the family results in more waste being produced. The more waste produced and placed in a landfill, the more methane is produced which is another common greenhouse gas. Promote and practise aforestation and reforestation.

Source: Adapted from "What is Climate Change?"
http://www.takepart.com/flashcards/what-is-climate-change/index.html

TASK EIGHT

Source 3

Estimated Rate of Tropical Deforestation, 1960-90

Figure 9.4

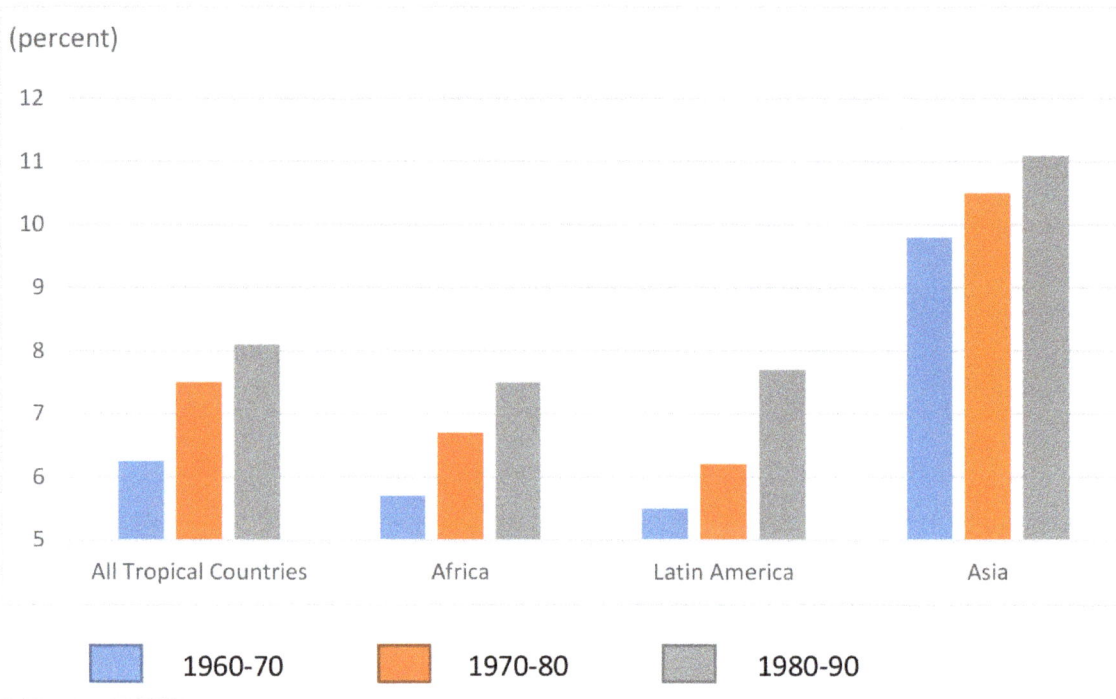

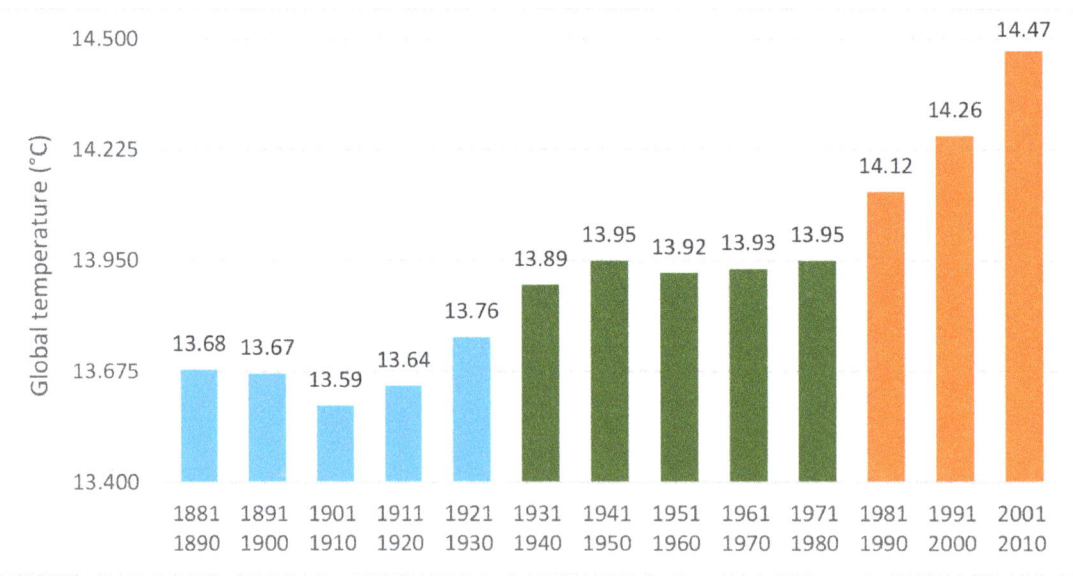

TASK EIGHT

Task 1

Describe the relationship between the graphs in Source 3.

_____
_____
_____
_____
_____
_____

Task 2

Read each statement and tick the source from which the information may be found.

Statements	Source 1	Source 2	Both source 1 and 2	Neither of the sources
Possible solution for climate change				
Causes of climate change				
Definition of climate change				
What can governments do to reduce global warming?				

TASK EIGHT

Task 3

On a visit to a friend in deep rural Hanover you met Havana. Havana does not attend school on Fridays because she helps her mother on her farm, then goes to the market with her to sell the produce. You noticed that they clear the land by burning. You mentioned that their action is contributing to climate change. Havana seems clueless. You have promised to give her information on climate change but had to leave in a hurry. You note her address and promised to write to her.

> **Plenty District, Lucea**
> **P.O. Box 447**
> **Hanover**

Using the information only from the sources write a letter to Havana, explaining what is climate change, three causes and three possible ways in which it can be mitigated.

Remember to include all the parts of a letter. Ensure that you obey the

C apitalization

O rganization

P unctuation

S equence

_____
_____
_____
_____
_____
_____
_____

TASK EIGHT

Task Nine

Source 1

Overpopulation is an undesirable condition where the number of existing human population exceeds the carrying capacity of Earth. Overpopulation is caused by a number of factors. Reduced mortality rate, better medical facilities and poor family planning are a few of the causes which result in overpopulation.

At the root of overpopulation is the difference between the overall birth rate and death rate in populations. If the number of children born each year equals the number of adults who die, then the population will stabilize. Talking about overpopulation shows that while there are many factors that can increase the death rate for short periods of time, the ones that increase the birth rate do so over a long period of time. The discovery of agriculture by our ancestors was one factor that provided them with the ability to sustain their nutrition without hunting. This created the first imbalance between the two rates.

Technological advancement was the biggest reason why the balance has been permanently disturbed. Science was able to produce better means of producing food, which allowed families to feed more mouths. Medical science has made many discoveries which were able to defeat a whole range of diseases. Illnesses that have claimed thousands of lives till now were cured because of the invention of vaccines. Combining the increase in food supply with fewer means of mortality tipped the balance and became the starting point of overpopulation.

Many people prefer to move to developed countries like the US, UK, Canada and Australia where best facilities are available in terms of medical, education, security and employment. The end result is that those people settle over there and those places have become overcrowded. The difference between the number of people who are leaving the country and the number of people who enter, narrows down which leads to more demand for food, clothes, energy and homes. This gives rise to the shortage of resources. Though the overall population remains the same, it just affects the density of population making that place simply overcrowded.

Source 2

The effects of overpopulation are quite severe. The first of these is the depletion of resources. The Earth can only produce a limited amount of water and food, which is falling short of the current needs. Most of the environmental damage being seen in the last fifty odd years is because of the growing number of people on the planet. They are cutting down forests, hunting wildlife in a reckless manner, causing pollution and creating a host of problems. Those engaged in talking about overpopulation have noticed that acts of violence and aggression outside of a war zone have increased tremendously while competing for resources.

With the overuse of coal, oil and natural gas, it has started producing some serious effects on our environment. The Rise in the number of vehicles and industries have badly affected the quality of air. The Rise in the amount of carbon dioxide emissions leads to global warming. Melting of The polar ice caps, changing climate patterns, rise in sea level are a few of the consequences that we might have to face due to environment pollution. The environment is definitely being degraded.

TASK NINE

Overpopulation in developing countries puts a major strain on the resources it should be utilizing for development. Conflicts over water are becoming a source of tension between countries, which could result in wars. It causes more diseases to spread and makes them harder to control. Starvation is a huge issue facing the world and the mortality rate for children is being fuelled by it. Poverty is the biggest hallmark we see when talking about overpopulation. All of this will only become worse if solutions are not sought out for the factors affecting our population. We can no longer prevent it, but there are ways to control it.

When a country becomes overpopulated, it gives rise to unemployment as there are fewer jobs to support a large number of people. Rise in unemployment gives rise to crime as people will steal to feed their family and provide their basic needs.

As the difference between demand and supply continues to expand due to overpopulation, it raises the prices of various commodities including food, shelter and healthcare. This means that people have to pay more to survive and feed their families.

Source 3

As the population of the world is growing at a rapid pace, raising the awareness among people regarding family planning and letting them know about the serious after effects of overpopulation can help curb population growth. One of the best ways is to let them know about various safe sex techniques and contraceptive methods available to avoid any unwanted pregnancy.

Imparting sex education to young children at the primary level should be a must. Most parents feel embarrassed in discussing such things with their children which result in their children going out to look for such information on the internet or discussing it with their peers. Mostly, the information is incomplete which results in sexually active teenagers unaware of contraceptives and embarrassed to seek information about same. It is therefore important for parents and teachers to shed their old inhibitions and make their children or students aware of solid sex education.

If the human population continues to grow rapidly, the effects of overpopulation on the environment will leave us with a planet that is no longer able to sustain us.

Source: https://www.conserve-energy-future.com/causes-effects-solutions-of-overpopulation.php

TASK NINE

Task 1

Use bullet points to write the main points from the sources.

Source 1	
Source 2	
Source 3	

TASK NINE

Task 2

Read each statement carefully then note (by ticking) if it is supported or not supported by the source(s).

Statement	Supported	Not Supported
Source 2 offers a definition for the term 'climate change'.		
Source 3 provides details of the causes of climate change.		
Three factors were given as causes for overpopulation.		
Possible solutions to overpopulation can be found in source 3.		
Urbanization was discussed as one major effect of overpopulation.		

TASK NINE

Task 3

Write two sentences from the sources that support the statement, "Over-population can only be lessened by a change in human behaviour"

_____
_____
_____
_____
_____
_____

Task 4

Compose a poem of two stanzas which inform about the impact of over-population on the environment.

Task Ten

Source 1

Bullying is a repeated aggressive behaviour characterized by a power imbalance and the intent to cause harm. Students who are bullied often feel threatened and powerless.

While bullying can be destructive and persistent, it can also be subtle enough that teachers are not aware of it. Since bullying can lead to long-lasting psychological, emotional, and physical problems, it is essential for teachers to recognize the signs of bullying and how to combat it.

The three types of bullying students can experience are direct bullying, indirect bullying, and cyber bullying. Within these categories lie verbal, physical, and social or relational bullying.

Direct bullying is a combination of both verbal and physical bullying. Verbal bullying involves spoken comments or written information that is emotionally damaging to the targeted student. Physical bullying consists of physically harming a student or their possessions. An example of direct bullying is hitting a student while also calling them rude names or using foul language.

Indirect bullying is mainly verbal and is experienced frequently in schools. An example of such behaviour involves one student spreading false information about another student aimed at causing embarrassment.

TASK TEN

The rise of technology has taken bullying to the internet. Cyber bullying is when students use email or social media platforms like Facebook to write damaging content. A common form of cyber bullying is sharing a student's private photos or videos without his/her consent. This form of bullying is more dangerous and often takes place off the school grounds, so it is more difficult for teachers to detect and address.

Similar to cyber bullying, social or relational bullying is when students gossip or spread rumours to hurt the reputation of the student being bullied.

Source 2

After conducting a study on possible causes of bullying, Mrs. Berry presented her findings to a group of Grade 6 students who have been bullied over aperiod of no less than six months.

- They believe that they are inferior and as a result launch an attack on those who appear to be confident so that they can feel good about themselves.
- Bullies who are confident lack compassion and empathy and respond in an aggressive manner if they feel threatened.
- Some bullies are seeking attention.
- Some want to be perceived as brave and get involved in acts that make them appear to be a hero.
- Some are dealing with issues such as abuse (physical and emotional), neglect or a broken family because of divorce.
- Some are angry and jealous of siblings. Their victims tend to have traits of the sibling or relative with whom they have a conflict.

Source 3

December 12, 2018

Dear Diary

I can't wait for the term to come to a close. I am sick and tired of these bullies. I hate them! I came to this school as an 'A' student and now I am classified as a poor performer. How can I focus and show interest when all I can think about are the lies other students have been spreading about me and my family. They don't even know my family members. They call me 'fatty'. They say I look like a barrel and I should be shaped like an hour glass. They have beaten me in the bathroom stalls and I have had to lie to my parents about the injuries.

That's not all!!! I now experience stomach aches and headaches, I think it is because of the fear I feel. I cannot sleep; I know I am depressed. I feel so powerless, so confused. I have been having suicidal thoughts and lately I have been thinking of a plan to physically harm, permanently damaging one, just one of the bullies to send a message. What message? I am tired of you; stop bullying me!

TASK TEN

Activity 1

Read each statement and tick the appropriate category.

Statement	Agree	Disagree
There are five types of bullying.		
If you post an unsightly picture of your classmate without consent that can be classified as social bullying.		
Bullies are dissatisfied with themselves and want their victims to feel inferior.		
The person who made the diary entry is experiencing cyber bullying.		
Signs of bullying were discussed in Source 1.		

Activity 2

Differentiate between social bullying and cyber bullying.

_____
_____
_____
_____
_____
_____
_____
_____
_____

Activity 3

Through which of the methods could Mrs. Berry have obtained the information for her study? Justify your reasons for selecting the ones you choose. **Observation, interviews, journal entries, surveys.**

_____
_____
_____
_____
_____
_____
_____
_____
_____

TASK TEN

Activity 4

You have stumbled upon the diary of the victim of bullying in Source 3 and read the entry made on December 12. You do not want to expose the person but want the staff members to pay close attention to him/her. Write a report to the principal of your school about the horrors the person has been enduring.

To: _____

From: _____

Date: _____

Subject: _____

Summary of Event:

_____
_____
_____
_____
_____
_____
_____
_____
_____
_____
_____
_____
_____
_____
_____
_____
_____

Task Eleven

Source 1

Plastic bags are everywhere in our environment. When we go to purchase our groceries, we use plastic bags because they are convenient. In fact, it has become part of us. However, the convenience of these plastic bags come at a very high cost to the environment and negatively affect human health. Several cities globally have begun banning the use of plastic bags while some have enforced restricted laws against the use of plastic bags because of the negative effects of their usage.

Birds, animals and marine life such as sea turtles and fish often mistake the plastic bag and other plastic materials for food and consume them. What happens once they consume these plastic materials is that their digestive system gets congested leading to the development of health infections and death when there is suffocation. The animals may also become easily entangled inside the plastic.

Plastic materials once released into the environment find their way into waterways and once they are there they dump into oceans. Great Pacific Ocean is one such area negatively affected with all the plastic material. The more they are thrown into the oceans the more they increase causing the garbage patch to increase in size. Plastic bags never degrade completely which shows that as more of them are produced by companies, then more are introduced into the environment. Banning the use of plastic bags will help reduce this great effect.

TASK ELEVEN

Source 2

As of January 1, 2019 the Government of Jamaica imposed a ban on single use plastic bags, straws and polystyrene. The ban covered the importation, manufacture and distribution of the materials.

The plastic bags banned are those that are commonly referred to as 'scandal bags' or other bags with dimensions of 24 inches by 24 inches or less.

Bags that are used for packaging and maintaining public health or food safety standards will not be banned. This applies to plastics that are essential for the maintenance of food and safety standards and include plastics used to package raw meat, flour, sugar, rice and baked goods, such as bread.

In some instances the use of plastic bags will be allowed. However, manufacturers will have to apply to the National Environment and Planning Agency (NEPA) for exemptions.

The polystyrene ban applies to those that are used as food and beverage containers. Regarding drinking straws, the ban will not apply to those that are used in medical facilities like hospitals or care homes for patients.

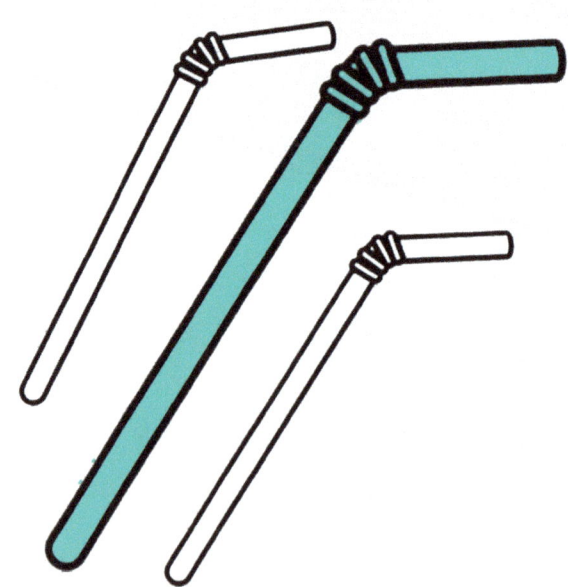

Source 3

From the impending Government ban on single-use plastic items, which was slated to take effect on January 1, 2019, a group of innovative, youthful, entrepreneurs has been gearing up to fill the imminent void.

The operators of Those Creative People Tings (TCP Tings), which is known for its signature line – 'One Bag Ah Tings', have created stylish tote bags to replace plastic or 'scandal' bags, normally used by consumers.

The bags, which were launched, are being marketed under the company's 'Scandal-Free' line, and provide consumers with a trendy and durable alternative to scandal bags. The bags may range from approximately $400 or more depending on the size. The bags sport a range of interesting branding depictions, which anticipated will serve to boost the government's drive to withdraw plastic bags from the market.

This may very well be a grate idea. but the implementation process was too swift. What about small business owners who still have the bags what were not sold! Should they dump them? Some consumers is not pleased and has complained that there plastic bags acted as garbage bags and only costed twenty dollars. One woman exclaimed, do the government accept us to get use to this."

TASK ELEVEN

Source 4

- Plastic bags pollute our water and also our land.
- The plastic bags are made from non-renewable sources and on this account, highly contribute to climate change.
- A lot of energy is used in producing these bags.
- Plastic bags help keep our streets clean.
- Plastic bags do not degrade readily.
- Plastic bags are harmful to wildlife and marine life. Plastic bags are harmful to human health.
- Plastic bags are expensive and hard to clean or remove from the environment.

Activity 1

a) Which word is used in all three sources as an adjective?

   (i) plastic   (ii) change   (iii) water   (iv) government

b) Which of the points in source 4 breaks the unity of the main idea being conveyed? Why did you choose that point?

   _____
   _____
   _____
   _____
   _____

c) Ms. Bennett asked two of her students to provide a title for Source 4.

   Raisean: Reasons for Banning Plastic

   Atlas: How to Save Money

TASK ELEVEN

With which of the two students would you agree? Justify your selection.

_____
_____
_____
_____
_____
_____

Activity 2

Reread the final paragraph in Source 3. Rewrite it making all necessary corrections related to grammar and punctuation.

_____
_____
_____
_____
_____
_____
_____
_____
_____
_____
_____
_____
_____
_____
_____
_____
_____

TASK ELEVEN

Activity 3

You overheard your aunt telling her friend that she does not care about what the government says about banning plastic bags. She has no intention of stopping its usage. You want to share some information with her about **the negative effects plastic bags have had on the environment** and the possible **benefits of banning their usage.** You are however afraid that if you do it face to face, she may interpret it as you acting like an adult. Write the letter.

_____
_____
_____
_____
_____
_____
_____
_____
_____
_____
_____
_____
_____
_____
_____
_____
_____
_____
_____
_____

Task Twelve

Source 1

The last sitting of the Grade Six Achievement Test was administered in March 2018. It is being replaced by The Primary Exit Profile (PEP)®. PEP will provide a profile of where the student is academically, the student's strengths and weaknesses, and their readiness for grade 7. PEP will assess students' knowledge, in addition to placing increased emphasis on assessing 21st century skills: collaboration, critical thinking, communication and creativity.

Unlike GSAT, this exam will assess more than just the content of mathematics, science, Language Arts and social studies. The new exam will have three components: ability test, performance task and curriculum based test. GSAT was administered over two days in the month of March, totalling approximately 6 hours. In GSAT students did language arts, mathematics, science, social studies and communication task. There were eighty multiple choice items in mathematics and language arts and sixty multiple choice items in science and social studies. The Communication Task paper included a completion of a form and one extended writing piece – narrative, persuasive, expository or descriptive. The extended piece could also be a report. PEP will run for five days, in three different months, totalling approximately eleven hours. Students will sit seven exams which will include a variety of question types including fill in the blanks, multiple choice, true or false, short answered items, among others.

Source 2

The examination has three components. Each will assess the children in different ways.

Ability Test

This component values **30%** of students' profile. It will measure students' ability to reason with words and quantities (Quantitative and Verbal Reasoning). The test will consist of **40** multiple choice items.

The Performance Task

This task is an activity that asks students to solve a problem by demonstrating their knowledge, understanding and ability. It is curriculum based and assesses how well students have grasped concepts from Language Arts and Mathematics. The scores for the Performance Tasks will be combined with the students' Mathematics and Language Arts scores from the Curriculum Based Tests to give the overall score of the students' achievement.

Curriculum Based Test

This component of PEP will assess students' knowledge of the content of Language Arts, Science, Social Studies and Mathematics at the Grade **6** level. Each subject will contain forty items. The types of questions will include multiple choice with one correct response, multiple choice with more than one answer and order matching. The science topics include the Environment, Light and Sound Energy, Properties and Uses of Materials, Human Body Systems and Mixtures. For Social Studies, students will measure how much students have gathered from the topics the Chinese and East Indians, showing honour and respect for our country, Mountains and Landmasses. Numbers, Measurement, Geometry, Data Handling Statistics and Algebra are the strands students will be tested on in mathematics. Grammar and Conventions, Comprehension, Vocabulary, Research/Study Skills will be assessed in Language Arts.

Source 3

PEP

I hate you and I wish you were never born!
I am frustrated, so very frustrated
"Classify, sequence, and critically think.
That's all you need to do," shouts my instructor without a blink

Cat is to kittens and dog is to puppies
Why should I care about these analogies?
There are items on age, time and shapes
And lots of figures for you to discriminate

I wish I were born earlier so I could do GSAT
For I am sure, to take my life, is PEP's plot
Synonyms, antonyms, homophones too
And all of seven tests! Lord, what did I do?

Oh well, I guess complaining won't make a difference
Since Leader Reid and the teachers have had a conference
I better start reading to build my vocabulary
Since to master PEP skills I have to work above the ordinary

Christine Fearon

TASK TWELVE

Activity 1

In Source 3, which figure of speech is dominantly used? Support your response with two lines from the poem.

_____
_____
_____
_____
_____
_____
_____
_____

Activity 2

In your opinion, which of the components will be least liked by Grade 6 students? Use information from the source to support your stance.

_____
_____
_____
_____
_____
_____
_____
_____
_____
_____
_____

TASK TWELVE

Your older cousin believes that PEP® is far easier than GSAT. You disagree. Using the information in all the sources, write an essay to persuade him/her that PEP is more demanding (requires more work) than GSAT.

Task Thirteen

Source 1

16 Zenith Drive,
Union Gardens,
Kingston 3
April 2, 2019

The Editor,
Jamaica Observer,
40 - 42½ Beechwood Avenue,
Kingston 5

Dear Mr. Allen:

I wish to provide a response regarding an article recently published in your newspaper ("Don't Return", March 30). The author, the president of the Jamaica Association for the Resettlement of Returning Residents, Percival LaTouche, urged Jamaicans overseas not to return home. According to LaTouche, "It makes no sense you spend 20, 30, or 40 years overseas working hard only to return home for people to take your life from you."

While his reasons for making such comments may be understood, I would like to shed some light on the implications associated with such a mandate. While he was not downright disrespectful or uncaring, it was evident that he did not consider the backlash his words could have on one of the most important industries.

TASK THIRTEEN

I would like to shed some more light on the impact associated with his instruction. While criminal acts affecting returning residents is a major cause for concern, the proposed solution is too hard and fast. Additionally, this can negatively affect the arrival of tourists to the island. If prospective returning residents are to remain abroad, what message are we sending to tourists?

Encouraging others to stay away from the country is a terrible approach to solving this problem. We need to educate criminals (I don't mean in a classroom) about the impact of their acts on the country's economy. I am sure they watch television. Advertisements can be used to inform them. Mr. Latouche's plan can put a huge dent in the tourist industry. Tourism has made a significant contribution to the Jamaican economy. It is the highest foreign exchange earner. Thousands of Jamaicans work directly or indirectly in tourism.

In fact, the tourist industry employs approximately two hundred thousand people, the second largest number of Jamaicans employed in any sector. They are employed in hotels, restaurants, transport, attractions, agriculture and craft.

Crime is a serious issue but we must be careful of the message we send while trying to combat it as this may have dire consequences on other industries.

Regards,

Randolph Johnson,
Concerned Businessman

TASK THIRTEEN

Source 2

Upon arriving in Jamaica, second time visitors (tourists) were asked the following question: **What is it about Jamaica that makes it your destination of choice despite the high crime rate?** Their responses are shown below.

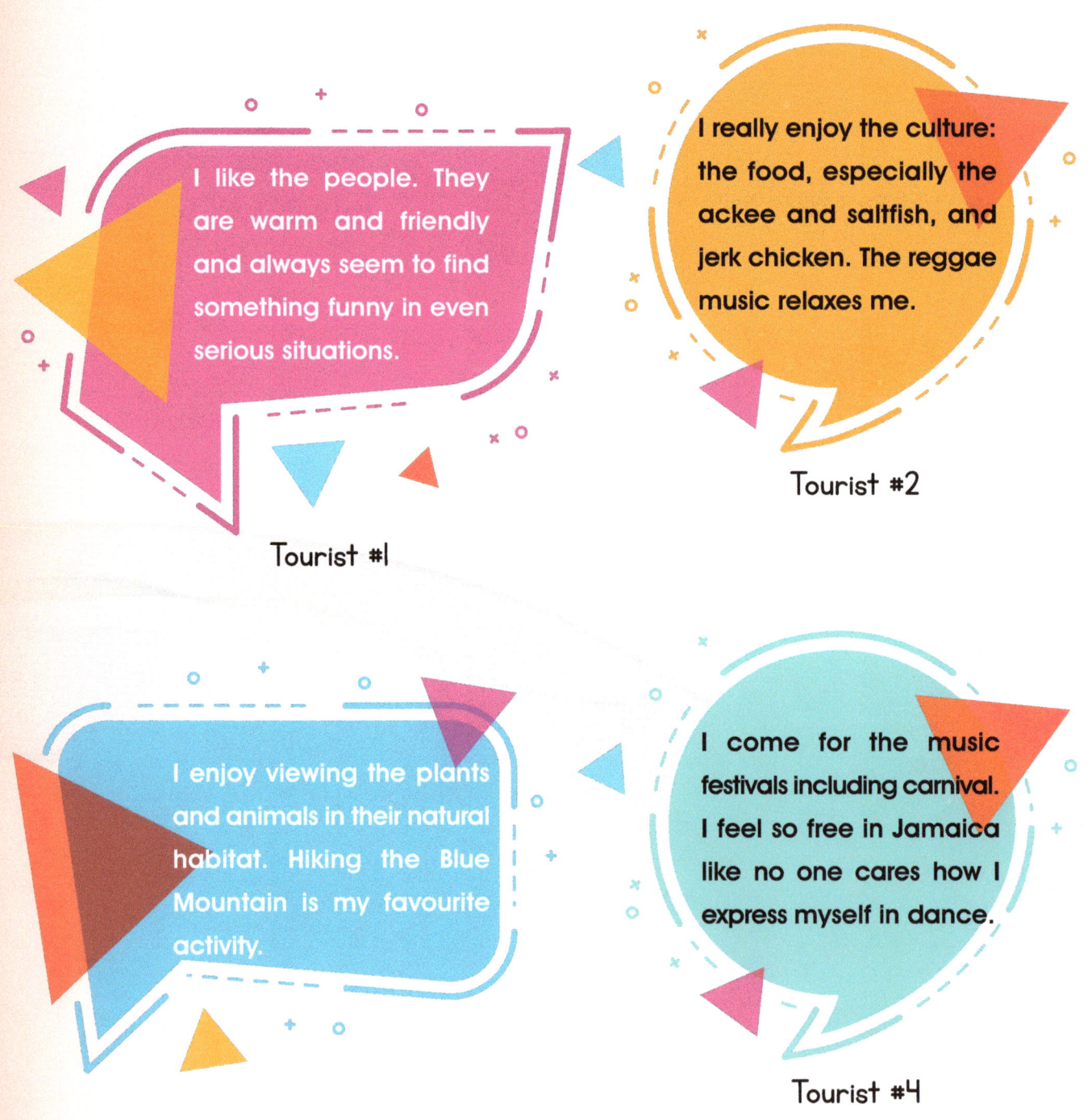

Tourist #1: I like the people. They are warm and friendly and always seem to find something funny in even serious situations.

Tourist #2: I really enjoy the culture: the food, especially the ackee and saltfish, and jerk chicken. The reggae music relaxes me.

Tourist #3: I enjoy viewing the plants and animals in their natural habitat. Hiking the Blue Mountain is my favourite activity.

Tourist #4: I come for the music festivals including carnival. I feel so free in Jamaica like no one cares how I express myself in dance.

TASK THIRTEEN

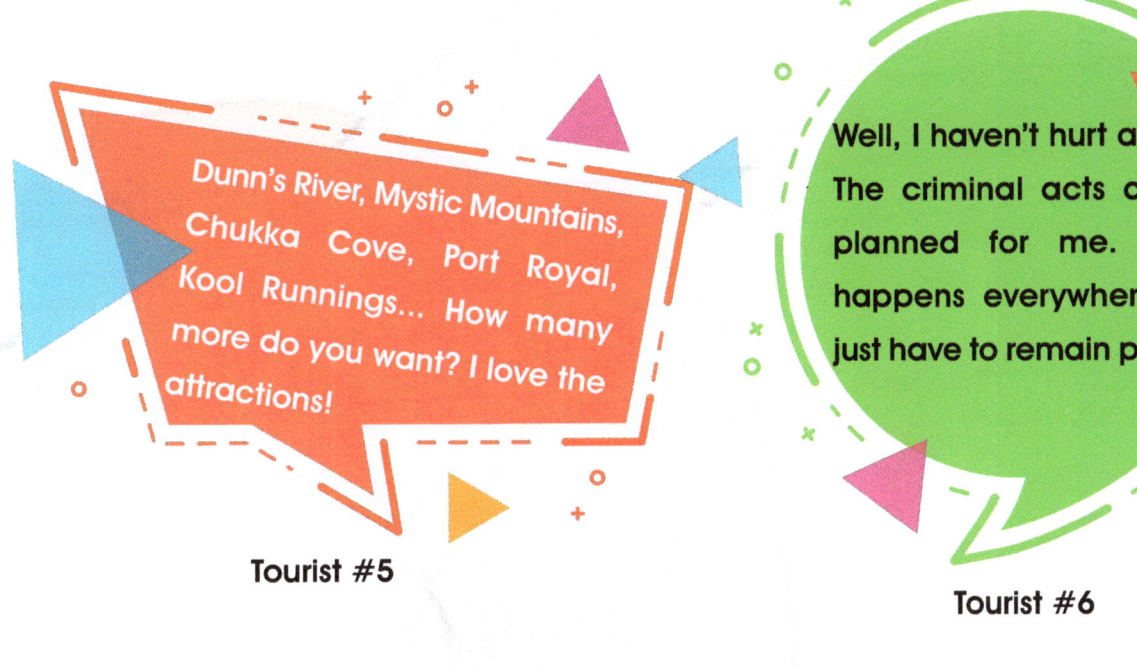

Tourist #5

Tourist #6

Part A

1) Which two details from source 1 indicate the writer agrees that there is a problem with crime?

   a) Criminal acts affecting returning residents is a major cause for concern.
   b) Encouraging others to stay away from the country is a terrible approach.
   c) This can negatively affect the arrival of tourists to the island.
   d) Crime is a serious issue.
   e) The tourist industry employs approximately two hundred thousand people

2) Which two tourists would most likely be eager to visit Black River Safari Trail?

   a) Tourist #1
   b) Tourist #2
   c) Tourist #3
   d) Tourist #4
   e) Tourist #5
   f) Tourist #6

TASK THIRTEEN

Part B

Read each statement carefully then indicate, by ticking, whether each is **supported** by Source 1 only, Source 2 only, Both Sources or Neither Source.

Statement	Source 1	Source 2	Both Sources	Neither Source
There are different reasons tourists come to Jamaica.				
More can be done by the government to reduce crime.				
The high crime rate affects the number of tourists visiting the island.				
The tourist industry is a major source of employment.				

Part C

TASK THIRTEEN

Write an essay **explaining three** reasons Jamaica is an ideal destination for tourists both at the regional and international level.

Be sure that you include the following:
- Introduction and conclusion
- Evidence to support the points you plan to explain
- Organize your essay into paragraphs
- Spelling, punctuation and grammar rules are to be observed

TASK THIRTEEN

TASK THIRTEEN

Task Fourteen

Source 1

Tobacco is a plant grown for its leaves, which are dried and fermented before being put in tobacco products. Tobacco contains nicotine, an ingredient that can lead to addiction, which is why so many people who use tobacco find it difficult to quit. There are also many other potentially harmful chemicals found in tobacco or chemicals that are created by burning it.

People can chew, smoke or sniff tobacco. Smoked tobacco products include cigarettes and cigars. Some people also smoke loose tobacco in a pipe or hookah (chillum pipe).

The nicotine in any tobacco product readily absorbs into the blood when a person uses it. Upon entering the blood, nicotine immediately stimulates the adrenal glands to release a special hormone. This special hormone fuels the central nervous system and increases blood pressure, breathing, and heart rate.

Although nicotine is addictive, most of the severe health effects of tobacco use comes from other chemicals. Tobacco smoking can lead to lung cancer, chronic bronchitis, and emphysema. It increases the risk of heart disease, which can lead to stroke or heart attack. Smoking has also been linked to other cancers, leukemia, cataracts, and pneumonia. All of these risks apply to use of anysmoked product, including hookah tobacco. Smokeless tobaccoincreases the risk of cancer, especially mouth cancers.

Smoking while pregnant may also be associated with learning and behavioral problems in exposed children. People who stand or sit near others who smoke are exposed to secondhand smoke. Secondhand smoke exposure can also lead to lung cancer and heart disease. It can cause health problems in both adults and children, such as coughing, mucus, reduced lung function, pneumonia, and bronchitis. Children exposed to secondhand smoke are at an increased risk of ear infections, severe asthma, lung infections, and death from sudden infant death syndrome.

Source 2

For many who use tobacco, long-term brain changes due to damages brought on by continued nicotine exposure result in addiction. When a person tries to desert the habit, he or she may have withdrawal symptoms, including the following: irritability, problems paying attention, trouble sleeping, increased appetite, powerful cravings for tobacco. Both behavioral treatments and medications can help people resign from smoking, but the combination of medication with counselling is more effective than either alone.

TASK FOURTEEN

Source 3

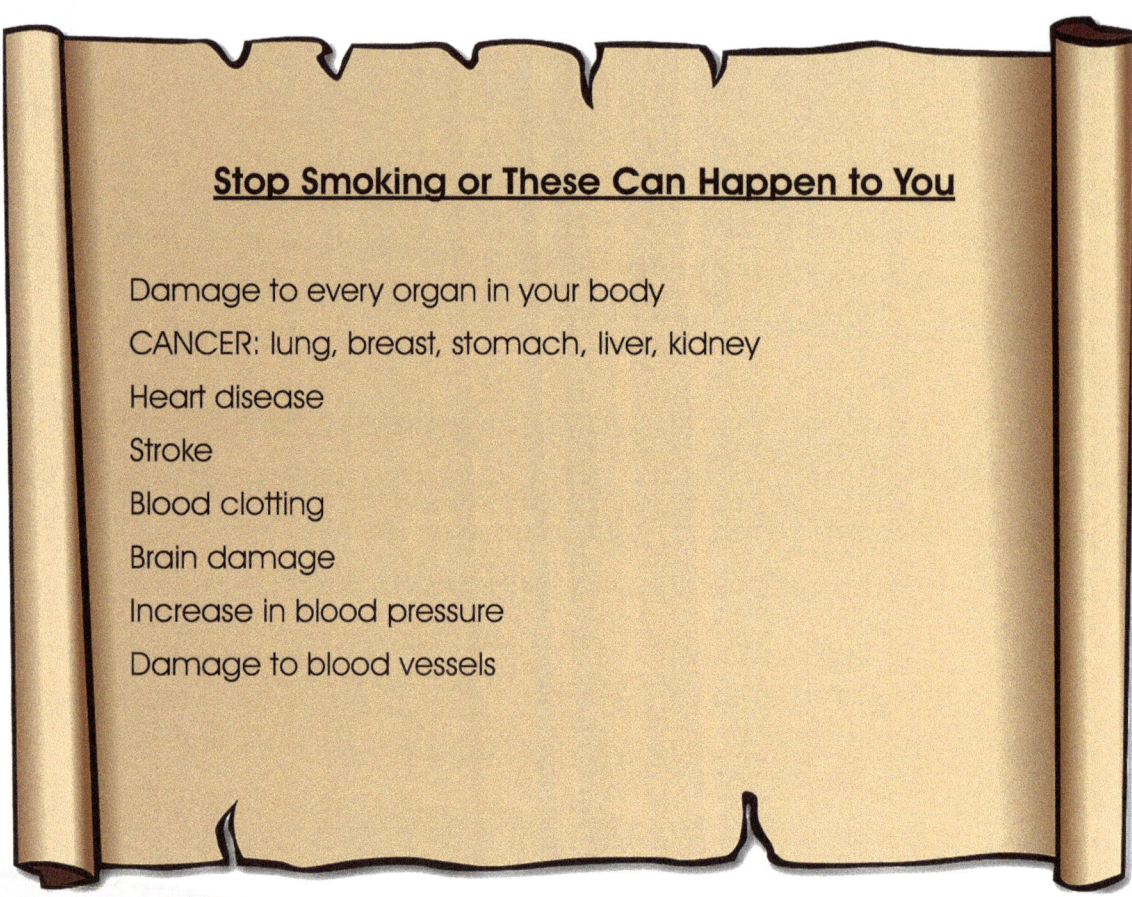

Stop Smoking or These Can Happen to You

Damage to every organ in your body
CANCER: lung, breast, stomach, liver, kidney
Heart disease
Stroke
Blood clotting
Brain damage
Increase in blood pressure
Damage to blood vessels

Part A
(CHOOSE ONE ITEM: EITHER 1 OR 2)

1) Which of the paragraphs in Source 1 could have the subtitle "How Do People Use Tobacco?"

   a) Paragraph 1
   b) Paragraph 2
   c) Paragraph 3
   d) Paragraph 4
   e) Paragraph 5

OR

TASK FOURTEEN

2) Which word in Source 2 could be replaced with **'quit'**
   a) effective
   b) exposure
   c) withdraw
   d) quit

Part B

Read each statement carefully then indicate, by ticking, the source(s) that has information to support each. You may tick more than one option if it applies.

Statement	Source 1	Source 2	Source 3	All three Sources
Tobacco can result in brain damage.				
Possible consequences of trying to stop the use of tobacco.				
Smoking does not only affect the person engaging in the act.				

TASK FOURTEEN

Part C

1) Create a jingle for an advertisement that would discourage people from smoking.

(2 marks)

TASK FOURTEEN

2) Horace Barrett is addicted to smoking cigarettes. You often see him sitting along the road taking a smoke. You want to know more about him and his commitment to smoking and possible reasons and if it affects his family. He has agreed to have you interview him. Write four questions you would ask him and then provide possible suitable responses. (4 marks)

Interviewer:
___

Horace:
___

Interviewer:
___

Horace:
___

Interviewer:
___

TASK FOURTEEN

Horace:

_____
_____
_____

Interviewer:

_____
_____
_____

Horace:

_____
_____
_____

Task Fifteen

StrongSport Company Limited has launched a new school bag and sent it to your school, Overachievers Primary, to get your thoughts about it. Each of the six children selected to be a part of the team wrote his/her review of the bag.

Jada: This bag is ideal for students at the primary level, high school and even college. I love the padded straps but I don't like that it only comes in red, blue or black.

Jaden – Ray: I like that the fabric is durable and water-proof. I really love the excellent padding in the straps. Additionally, it has many compartments to keep students organized, including a padded sleeve for laptops. The only downside is that it is missing extra support straps around the waist.

Jayden: It is the most spacious bag I have seen for my age group. It has all of the design features children my age need (organizing compartments and a chest strap). The material doesn't seem to be worn easily and will keep its original appearance for a long time.

TASK FIFTEEN

Jhemar: The fabric is made of recycled polyester. This is good for the environment. It also has an extra loop so children can attach a lunch bag and be hands-free.

Jonathan: It held all my books with room to spare. That's a whole lot of books because I am in Grade 6

Jori: Although it is spacious, I think it is too plain for girls. I would have endorsed this product if there were more colours that appeal to girls – colours like pink, orange and yellow.

Source 2

Whether they're heading to class, travelling during the holiday or going on job interviews, this versatile backpack has everything a college student needs: tons of pockets to stay organized including a separate laptop compartment, a built-in USB port to add a battery and charge devices on the go, and lots of padding to make it comfortable. It's not only spacious but the fact that the material used is recyclable is a major plus.

It also has a zippered pocket against the back for valuables and waterproof materials to help the contents stay safe. The absence of a chest strap is a welcome bonus; no college student, certainly not me, wants to walk around with a strap around the waist. It's simply not a 'cool' look.

It is a **Megazon** best-seller with over 3,000 positive reviews from users who swear it's both useful and professional. It is perfect as during the summer as a bottle compartment is there so we can keep hydrated.

The best part about this bag is the price. With so many desired features, it is only being sold at US $40.00 which is equivalent to approximately JM$5500. That's a small price for such a durable, valuable item that has the potential to last at least five years if properly cared for. Given the available colours, much washing will not be required. When the need arises use cold water on the gentle cycle.

I recommend this bag to parents of children at all levels especially those who carry laptop computers.

Part A

1) Source 2 was most likely written by a _____.

   a) parent
   b) student at the secondary level
   c) student at the primary level
   d) student at the tertiary level

2) After the review some four of the six students eagerly asked their parents to purchase one of the StrongSports bags. Which two students would least likely have asked?

   a) Jada
   b) Jaden-Ray
   c) Jayden
   d) Jhemar
   e) Jonathan
   f) Jori

TASK FIFTEEN

3) In the space provided, create a poster to advertise the StrongSport bag. Ensure to include all necessary information including locations where it is available.

TASK FIFTEEN

Part B

You have been asking your parents to purchase you a StrongSport school bag. They have expressed that they are not able to spend so much money on one bag. Write a letter to one of your parents convincing him or her to purchase the bag.

Be sure to include at least three relevant points to convince the parent (information from the sources); use appropriate punctuation and grammar; ensure that all the parts of the letter are included.

TASK FIFTEEN

Rubric for extended writing tasks: Narratives

RUBRIC FOR EXTENDED WRITING TASKS: NARRATIVES

6)
- Correct spelling, punctuation and capitalization; proper use of grammar; errors made do not interfere with a clear understanding.
- Sequenced logically and is clear; good word choice.
- Relevant to the topic; ideas sufficiently developed; expresses a sense of completeness.

5)
- Relevant to topic; ideas developed, there is a sense of completeness.
- Interesting word choice; logical progression of ideas and the sequence is clear.
- Few errors in spelling, punctuation and capitalization; proper use of grammar; errors made do not interfere with a clear understanding.

4)
- Fairly focused on topic; moderately developed ideas; conveys a sense of completeness.
- Sequence fairly clear; lapses may occur in organization; adequate word choice.
- Mostly correct spelling, punctuation and capitalization; few errors in grammar and usage; errors do not prevent understanding.

3)
- A basic focus on the topic; ideas are vague; loosely related material/content; conveys some sense of completeness.
- Organization attempted; sequence generally clear; engaging at times; occasionally vague word choice.
- Generally correct spelling, punctuation and capitalization; some errors in usage of grammar; errors do not prevent understanding.

2)
- Somewhat related to topic; insufficient development of ideas; loosely related content; lacks sense of completeness.
- Little evidence of organizational pattern; sequence is unclear.

RUBRIC FOR EXTENDED WRITING TASKS: NARRATIVES

- Some errors in spelling, punctuation and capitalization; errors prevent understanding.

1)
- Slightly focused on topic; very little development of ideas; lacks a sense of completeness.

- No organization and the sequence is unclear.

- Errors in spelling, punctuation and capitalization; frequent errors in use of grammar; errors made prevent a clear understanding.

0/Cannot be scored

- No focus on topic; no development of ideas; incomplete.

- No attempt at organization; no sequence; incorrect word choice;

- Critical errors in spelling, punctuation and capitalization/below the grade level; critical grammatical errors/below the grade level; errors prevent understanding.

Rubric for Persuasive Writing

RUBRIC FOR PERSUASIVE WRITING

6)
- Well focused on topic; clear position stated; many facts presented to support position; convincing arguments; sense of completion.
- Logically organized with reasons presented in clear order; clearly contains beginning, middle and end; easy to follow arguments.
- Correct spelling, punctuation and capitalization; proper use of grammar; errors made do not interfere with a clear understanding.

5)
- Focused on topic; clear position stated; ample support; presents convincing arguments; sense of completion.
- Logically organized with reasons presented in clear order; clearly contains beginning, middle and end; easy to follow arguments.
- Few errors in spelling, punctuation and capitalization; proper use of grammar; errors made do not interfere with a clear understanding.

4)
- Fairly focused on topic; position apparent; adequate support, though it may be uneven; may include loosely related content; presents convincing arguments; some sense of completion.
- Apparent organization but some lapse may occur; vaguely contains beginning, middle and end; fairly easy to follow arguments.
- Mostly correct spelling, punctuation and capitalization; few errors in grammar and usage; errors do not prevent understanding.

3)
- Fairly focused on topic; position may be apparent; some support included but inconsistent development; includes loosely related content; presents mediocre arguments; some sense of completion.
- Organization attempted; attempts to contain beginning, middle and end; generally easy to follow arguments.
- Generally correct spelling, punctuation and capitalization; some errors in usage of grammar; errors do not prevent understanding.

2)
- Somewhat related to topic; position may be unclear; inadequate support; includes loosely related content; lacks sense of completeness.
- Little evidence of organizational pattern; somewhat difficult to follow argument.

RUBRIC FOR PERSUASIVE WRITING

- Some errors in spelling, punctuation and capitalization; errors prevent understanding.

1)
- Slightly focused on topic; position unclear; very little development of support; lacks a sense of completeness.

- No organization; difficult to follow argument.

- Errors in spelling punctuation and capitalization; frequent errors in use of grammar; errors made prevent a clear understanding.

0/Cannot be scored

- No focus on topic; no position taken; no development of support; incomplete.

- No attempt at organization is present; cannot follow argument.

- Critical errors in spelling, punctuation and capitalization/below the grade level; critical grammatical errors/below the grade level; errors prevent understanding.

Rubric for Expository Writing

RUBRIC FOR EXPOSITORY WRITING

6)
- Well focused on topic; ideas supported with interesting details; sense of completion.
- Logical progression of ideas; strong topic sentence; excellent transition; easy to follow.
- Correct spelling, punctuation and capitalization; proper use of grammar; errors made do not interfere with a clear understanding.

5)
- Focused on topic; ideas supported with details; sense of completion.
- Logical progression of ideas; good topic sentence; good transition; easy to follow.
- Few errors in spelling, punctuation and capitalization; proper use of grammar; errors made do not interfere with a clear understanding.

4)
- Fairly focused on topic; ideas adequately supported but development may be uneven; may include loosely related content; some sense of completion.
- Apparent organization but some lapse may occur; adequate topic sentence; some transition; fairly easy to follow.
- Mostly correct spelling, punctuation and capitalization; few errors in grammar and usage; errors do not prevent understanding.

3)
- Fairly focused on topic; some loosely related content; adequate details included but inconsistent development.
- Organization attempted; few transitions; adequate topic sentence; generally easy to follow arguments.
- Generally correct spelling, punctuation and capitalization; some errors in usage of grammar; errors do not prevent understanding.

2)
- Somewhat related to topic; inadequate details; includes loosely related content; lacks sense of completeness.

RUBRIC FOR EXPOSITORY WRITING

- Little evidence of organizational pattern; weak topic sentence; somewhat difficult to follow.

- Some errors in spelling, punctuation and capitalization; errors prevent understanding.

1)
- Slightly focused on topic; inadequate details; lacks a sense of completeness.

- No organization; topic sentence not evident; difficult to follow.

- Errors in spelling, punctuation and capitalization; frequent errors in use of grammar; errors made prevent a clear understanding.

0/Cannot be scored

- No focus on topic; no development of ideas; incomplete.

- No attempt at organization is present; cannot follow.

- Critical errors in spelling, punctuation and capitalization/below the grade level; critical grammatical errors/below the grade level; errors prevent understanding.

www.ingramcontent.com/pod-product-compliance
Lightning Source LLC
Chambersburg PA
CBHW060935170426
43194CB00026B/2964